Through the Eyes of Jesus

Volume 1

by C. Alan Ames

1st printing, Oct. 1996 — 20,000 copies
2nd printing, July 1997 — 20,000 copies

Printed and Distributed in the U.S.A. by:

The 101 Foundation, Inc.
P.O. Box 151
Asbury, New Jersey 08802-0151

Phone: 908-689 8792
Fax: 908-689 1957

Dedication

To my wife, Kathryn, who has supported me with her love, and in fond memory of Bernard Nesden, a good friend, who devoted his life to God.

Books available from the 101 Foundation and also from:

New Zealand
Patrick J. Clegg
P. O. Box 31495
Lower Hutt
New Zealand
Phone & Fax: 644 566 5786

Ireland
Touch of Heaven
66 Landscape Park
Churchtown
Dublin 14, Ireland
Phone & Fax: 01-298 5403

England
Angelus Communications
22 Milbury Drive
Littleborough
Lancashire OL15 OBZ
England
Phone & Fax: 01706 372 674

Australia
Touch of Heaven
P. O. Box 85
Wembley
Western Australia 6014
Phone 09-275 6608
Fax: 619-382 4392

ISBN # 1-890137-00-6

Preface

by C. Alan Ames
July 27, 1996

The Lord God, Jesus Christ, has been speaking and appearing to me in visions since February, 1994. At first I did not write anything down, but later I was asked by God to take up a pen and record what I was experiencing. Then, on the sixth of February, 1996, Jesus started to show me some episodes of His life on earth.

Through His eyes, I began to see singular incidents that took place as He traveled with His disciples through the towns and villages in the Holy Land. While this was happening, He also granted me the grace to perceive His thoughts.

As I saw and heard these scenes of God's love before me, I was often overwhelmed with tears of sadness or joy. It seemed that at each revelation there was a lesson to be learned and pondered upon, for by revealing these events He was teaching us how to live and to love.

In Judas, I began to see all the weaknesses that so many of us have and, when we ignore or forget God, who is always with us and ready to help us, how easy it is to be lead away from Him. In Judas, I was also shown that the Lord Jesus will forgive any mistakes we make in life, because He loves us so much. All we need to do is to accept His love and to ask for His forgiveness.

The temptations, feelings, problems, and desires of men at that time were much the same as those of today. Perhaps one reason that the Lord is giving these insights is to show us that it is possible to conquer self and to conquer sin. We need only to call upon God, as His help is never failing. "Ask and thou shalt receive." In these passages, He shows us the way.

The visions and words continue.

Editor's Note, (Dr. Rosalie A. Turton, Director, 101 Foundation)

Scripture tells us, "And I suppose that if all the other events in Jesus' life were written, the whole world could hardly contain the books!" (John 21:23).

In our times, we have been privileged to be able to read the private revelations of Venerable Anne Catherine Emmerich, St. Bridget of Sweden, Abbess Maria Cecilia Baij, Maria Valtorta, Luisa Piccarreta, Venerable Mary of Agreda, and others, telling us some of the incidents which may have occurred in the lives of Jesus and the saints. Once again we are blessed with some private revelations about the life of Jesus, given by Him to Carver Alan Ames.

In time, the Church will judge the authenticity of these revelations. We do not attempt to preempt the Church in this matter, but whether or not these events actually took place, what is important is that this book provides spiritual reading which raises our minds and thoughts to God and illustrates ways to change our own lives to become holier.

Whatever we may do, this is our true occupation on earth. To become holier...to become instruments of God and thus save ourselves and help to save others. To this end, we place these words in print for your edification and spiritual growth.

Below is a sample of the text taken from the revelations of February 20, 1996, to whet your appetite for what is to follow in these pages:

The sound of horses and men marching quickly could be heard and then a garrison of Roman soldiers passed us heading for the village. The clatter of their weapons and the stamping of their feet almost deafened us as they passed.

When we arrived at the village it was in turmoil. The soldiers had searched the houses for rebels and had arrested five men whom they were treating harshly. The villagers were gathered around begging the Romans to free the men. They proclaimed the innocence of the men and called for their release. The Centurion on his horse would not listen and ordered his soldiers to push the crowd back.

As they did, a young boy broke free and ran forward crying, "Father, father." A large burly soldier hit the child very hard with his closed fist and the young boy, who was about four years old, fell to the ground and began to convulse. The crowd became silent as the officer boomed to the soldier, "You fool, he is only a child!"

The officer jumped from his horse and leaned over the child who had stopped convulsing and was now dead. As he removed his helmet, tears were seen running down his face and he cried, "He is only a child, a baby. My son is this age, a baby." He began to sob from his heart.

I walked forward as the crowd parted to make way for Me. The soldiers looked as if to stop Me when someone shouted, "It is Jesus of Nazareth, the great prophet, the great healer." Hearing this, the soldiers stood back and I went to the child. The Centurion looked at Me and said, "Can You help?" In his heart I could see a lost soul, one full of the pain of the work he did, full of death and destruction...but hidden behind this confusion, I could also see compassion, love, and hope.

"I will," was My reply as I leaned forward and picked up the child. "But he is dead," said the soldier who had hit the boy. "There is nothing You can do now." I gave him a soft smile and said, "My Father, Who sent Me, saves or takes life. It is His to command...and if it is His will that this child lives, then he will live."

"Then Your Father must be a magician," said the soldier. "No, My Father is the God of Creation Who made all things and it *is* His will that this child lives." As I said this, the child awoke crying, "Mother!"

The soldier stood back amazed as the child's mother came and took him...full of joy, full of thanks, and praising God for His mercy. The soldiers were still staring at Me as the crowd began to praise God in unison. "Who are You?" shouted a soldier in fear. "I Am," I said, and the crowd became silent. "What sort of an answer is that? I asked who You are, and You say, 'I Am.'"

"I am the Son, I am the Lamb, and I am the forgiveness of God." The Centurion jumped on his horse nervously and snapped at his men, "Set those prisoners free. We do not want them." He looked at Me and gave a nod of thanks as he rode off leading his men from the village.

†††

1.

Jesus ††† 2-6-96

As we walked along the path to the next village, my disciples were discussing the events that had just happened in the last town. Peter was shouting My praises saying, "Truly, our Master is the Messiah. Look at all the miracles that happen. Look at all the people healed. Look at all the love Jesus shares. Truly, He is the Lord."

James and John agreed, and full of excitement and joy, they started to dance and sing, "The Lord has come, the Lord has come." There were many discussions among the others all praising God and talking of God's love.

As we approached the next village James ran forward and asked, "Master, will there be any miracles here today?" I looked at him, so young, so innocent, so full of love, and so trusting. How I wished all mankind could be as he is.

I said to James, "Miracles happen where faith is strong. Miracles happen to strengthen the faith, to bring people back to God, and to save souls. If in this town a miracle is needed, it will happen." James looked at Me and smiled, filled with expectation of what would happen.

"Lord," a voice called, "where will we stay and how will we buy food, for we only have a few coins...not enough to feed us. Maybe we should ask the people to pay when You heal them." I answered Judas, "What I give, I give to glorify God, I give in the name of the Father, and I give freely."

"How, then, will we eat? Tell me that."

Poor Judas did not really understand. He thought not with his heart but with his head, and always with his pocket.

"Trust in Me, Judas, I will supply all we need. My Father in Heaven will give all that is needed so that His wishes will be fulfilled. I fed the five thousand, do you not believe that I can feed us?"

Judas, in frustration and doubt, went off mumbling and complaining to others.

Just then a shout was heard, "He comes, He is here. It is the Prophet. It is Jesus the Nazarene.

Bring out the sick, bring them out. He is here. He will cure them!" The village came to life; people running from house to house telling their neighbors I was there. Within no time there was a crowd pushing and shoving to get close to Me.

I stood upon a rock and asked them to sit and taught them thus: "The Father in Heaven has sent Me to heal your hearts, to mend your souls, and to show you the truth of Yahweh. The Father in His endless mercy offers you His love and forgiveness, offers you eternal peace, eternal joy, and eternal love. Look at your children and see how much you love them and want the best for them in life. As they grow, you guide them, advise them, and help them to develop into the true children of God they were meant to be. The Father in Heaven is your Father and He looks upon you, only wanting to guide, to help, and to advise, so that the rewards of Heaven are yours.

"See a person making bread. They put in the correct mixture and then knead it until it is right to bake. With the warmth of the fire, the bread rises to be what it was made to be. God's children are the same. The Father gives you all you need to rise to your full potential, then He offers you the fire of His love, through the Holy Spirit, to warm you, to set the oven of your soul alight, so that you can become what you are supposed to be. All you have to do is to open the doors of your hearts to let the warmth of God fill you and bring you to eternal peace."

J
e
J e s u s
u
s

Jesus ††† 2-7-96

I opened My arms wide and said, "All those in need, find it in Me...all those in pain, be freed through Me...all those who are lost, be found by Me. I am the Light come into the world to lift mankind's burdens. I am the Light that shines in the dark. I am the Light sent by the Father to show the way."

3.

The crowd rushed forward trying to touch Me... trying to be near Me. Peter, in a strong voice, ordered them to wait in turn and, one by one, I touched them and asked the Father to lift their pains. The blind saw, the deaf heard, the crippled walked.

A little child came forward, and I saw that one of his legs was much shorter than the other. Holding his mother's hand, oh so tight, he stumbled forward.

"Rabbi, please touch my son, please heal him. He was born this way and it must be that he is paying for my sins. Please Rabbi, heal him. Ask of me what you will and I will give it, but please heal my innocent son." She broke into tears and her son embraced her and started to sob, "Mother, don't cry, I love you. Mother, please don't cry."

My heart broke to see such sorrow and to see so much love. How could I not answer her pleas?

"Child, come to Me," I said. The child looked hesitantly at Me. "Come," I said.

Nervously he hobbled forward and I reached down and picked him up. As I embraced him, I kissed away his tears and called to the Father, "Father, You have sent Me to do Your will, so now to glorify You, I set this child free in Your name."

When I placed the child on the ground he was cured and his legs were even. All the people began shouting praises to God, and his mother kissed My feet. I raised her up and said, "Now you know the love of God. Bring your child up as an offering for God's glory."

The crowd grew and grew and I saw My disciples becoming weary, as I was. I said to Peter, "It is time to go." He wondered where. Then a voice called out, "Master, come to my house and rest." I looked and saw the face of an old man, and in his face I could see his soul, which was full of the love of God. "Thank you, it is a welcome offer." And so we went.

When we arrived at his house the disciples were all almost asleep, but he presented such a wonderful meal we could not refuse. Over the table he said, "Today I have seen the hand of God at work. Today the Messiah has graced our village. Today I will never forget."

Judas turned to him and said, "I hope that the villagers do not forget to reward the Master appropriately."

"Judas," I said in a loud voice, "it is reward enough to share a banquet and to have such a wonderful host. The people gave reward enough with their praise of God."

"But, Master, we have so little money!"

Peter, My trusted friend, cut in, "If the Master says we have enough then it is so. Do not bother Him again."

Judas, embarrassed, turned away with anger in his eyes. In his heart I could see the turmoil, the anger, the wish for revenge.

"Judas, My friend, do not take it so. You know I hold you dear to Me, and it saddens Me to see you hurt." He looked at Me with love for a moment and then confusion, saying, "Yes Master, I know," then turned away in self pity.

Our host turned to Me and said, "My Lord, today my soul has felt the love of God. How can I ever forget this? Now I can welcome death when it comes, for I know the joy that awaits me there."

"The joy in Heaven was there for you already," I replied, "but it is true that you have tasted its sweetness today. Your life has been looked upon by My Father from the day you were born. Your love of God, through adversity and through pain, has been a gift welcomed in Heaven. My Father has set a place for you at His table, where we will sit and enjoy each other's company throughout eternity. Old man, your heart belongs to God, and so your rewards are with God."

The next day as we left, people came running forward and placed money and food in My disciples' hands saying, "Please come back. Come back soon." Judas looked happy.

The day was hot and dusty and so after awhile we sat to rest. Matthew came forward with John. "Master, You must rest more. You do so much but take so little time to rest. Whenever someone calls, You are there without thought for Yourself. You must rest or You will be sick."

In reply, I said, "My time is set in stone. My days are numbered. When I return to My Father, it will be on the day He calls and in the way He asks, and I must go alone. Until then, I will do My Father's work at all times to build the new people of God. In the next village there is a tavern. Go ahead and arrange a room for three days so that I may rest, as I will in the future. Then in three days, I will arise fresh and strong to do My Father's will."

The tavern room was small but quiet and comfortable. For three days I slept peacefully, and on the third day I awoke feeling close to My Father. There was a bang on the door: "Master, are You awake? Come quickly." It was James full of excitement, as usual. I went outside and saw in the tavern a Roman soldier who had been attacked by a Zealot. He had a wound in his heart, and everyone thought he would die.

"Cure him please Master, lest the Roman garrison comes for revenge," cried the innkeeper. I looked at the soldier; he was a Centurion, a commander of men. I saw no fear of death in his eyes, only concern for his family. "This man I will heal, not to prevent revenge but for the love he carries in his heart for his family and to bring his heart to God." I laid My hand on his wound and it closed. He arose and said, "Holy Man, I will not forget You and I will pray to my gods for Your success."

With love, I answered, "There is no god but God, and I am the Son sent to free the world from its false gods, false idols, and false values."

"I do not understand You Holy Man, but I feel good when You talk and it seems to me that You speak the truth. Who is this God?" he asked.

"It is My Father in Heaven who only wants goodness for all, who loves all, and who calls all His family. I come to testify to His greatness, His love, His power, and His mercy."

Falling to his knees he cried, "Lord, I hear and believe. From now on I only want to know Your Father as my God and You as Lord. Let me stay and follow You. Let me help."

"My friend," I replied, "you need to return to your family, for they wait for you. Now in all you do, show love to all; hurt no one...only help. Live each day as an offering of thanks to the Father and in this way you will follow Me and walk the path to eternal joy."

He left full of love, full of hope, and full of promise. From that day forth until the day he came to Heaven, he kept his word and lived his life for God.

My disciples were amazed, saying, "Lord, he is a gentile, a Roman, how could You promise him Heaven?" Lovingly I turned to them and said, "I am the Light for the world; I save all who want to be saved, be they Jew or gentile, for the Father created all peoples and loves all peoples, and I, as His Son, share that love."

J
E
J E S U S
U
S

Jesus ††† 2-8-96

As we left the inn a crowd gathered, and some cried out, "Jesus, touch me...Jesus, heal me...Jesus, help me." Always there were those in need coming to Me for help, and always I longed to respond, for I loved them all. I asked My disciples to gather the people in the market place.

As they sat, a hush came over the crowd. I stood before them and said, "One day a man came to the temple and fell to his knees. He cried out to the Father to help him in his hour of need. His crops had failed and he didn't know how he would feed his family. The man promised God he would live his life helping others if God would help him this time.

"The Father in His mercy heard him and answered his prayer. When the man returned home he found that an inheritance had arrived for him. His uncle died and left him a vast fortune. The man was happy, although not thinking of his uncle who died or of his promise to God. He sold his property and moved into his uncle's mansion, living a life of the wealthy, spoiling his family, and enjoying life among his new found friends.

"One day his former neighbor was at his door asking for help, as his crops had failed. The wealthy man would not open his door to his old neighbor, and told his servants to chase him away. As he heard his servants doing his will, the wealthy man remembered how he had begged God to help him, and that God had answered. Shouting to his servants, he said, 'Tell him to go to the temple and ask for God's help, as I did; God has plenty for all.' Feeling pleased with himself he went to sleep. The poor neighbor listened to the words and went to the temple and asked God for help. He also asked God to forgive the wealthy man who had not helped him.

"Now it came to pass that the wealthy man lost his property during an invasion and was being sought by the invading warriors. In the middle of the night, lost and alone, the wealthy man stumbled into the farm of the poor neighbor. He cried, 'Help me, my friend, they are out to kill me.'

"The poor man said, 'Even though you did not know, it was you who helped me when I was in need, by reminding me to trust in God. I forgave you and asked God to forgive your selfishness. Now in thanks for God's mercy to me, I will do what I can to help you.'

"At that moment the wealthy man understood that the poor man had the true riches in his trust and love for God. He threw himself on the ground and begged God's forgiveness for being so blind. In repentance he spent his remaining years serving the poor man and praising God.

"Do you understand the lesson today? It is this: when you ask for God's help you must remember that He answers your prayers. And in turn when you are asked for help, you must do likewise. In this way praise the Lord for His love and mercy in your life."

"Master, how can we help each other when we have so little to share," someone asked? "The Romans and tax collectors take most of what we have."

"It is not only in goods you must share, but also in love and in prayers," I replied. "The greatest gift that you can give your brothers and sisters is to share your love with them."

A Pharisee stood up and said, "You have said to share our love and I say 'well said,' but what about the tithes we pay to the temple? In times of need, should we refuse to pay these and keep the money to share among ourselves?" I could see the trickery in his heart.

"You would have Me say, 'Do not make your offerings to God,' and then condemn Me for saying so. I say to you, in times of need, all God asks is what you can give; all God asks is your love; all God asks is your trust. David ate the food of the temple to survive and to do God's will. Since the Father loves all men, do you think He would deny anyone his needs? You Pharisees sit in wealth, in places of esteem, in thoughts of self, and declare to others how they must live to God's laws. Look to yourselves first and see how you must live to God's laws." The Pharisee left quickly to tell his friends of My words.

The sick came forward, and there were so many that I could not touch them all. I blessed My followers and gave them God's power to heal. United as one love, we touched many and many were healed. As the evening fell, we left the village and found a secluded place to rest.

J
e
J e s u s
u
s

Jesus ††† 2-10-96

Through the night, we sat around a fire that we had made behind a wall in a meadow. We talked about the day's events, and then My disciples fell asleep. As they slept I looked upon their faces, and each one, in some way, showed Me a different aspect of mankind's struggle to come to the Father. I looked into the heart of Judas and knew what was to come, and it saddened Me for I loved him so. To look upon

Judas, I was looking upon so many who had denied, and would deny and even betray their loving Father in Heaven. My heart became heavy with such thoughts, and I drifted into the embrace of a welcomed sleep.

The day broke with the birds singing a joyful song, their sweet voices uniting in harmony to praise God. The freshness of the early morning air filled My lungs with the taste of the Father's pure creation. One by one My followers awoke, and after cleansing themselves, began to prepare a meal. James in his boyish ways was running around playing with his companions. When he came to Judas, he playfully embraced him. Judas turned sharply saying, "Boy, go and do something useful. See if the Master needs anything. Stop your childishness."

Peter came over and said to Me, "Lord, why do You allow such a man to follow You, for he shows so little love?"

"Peter, do you not understand yet that I love you all; I love you and want to guide you in the Way. Judas needs more help than you others, but this does not mean that I should ignore or reject him. His soul is as precious to Me as any other, and I will not deny him My love."

"Master, how can You continue to accept his bad temper, his greed, and yes, his jealousy? He seems to be constantly disagreeing with Your wishes. He tries to get You to do his will, and yet You do not send him away. I do not understand this," said Peter.

"Oh, Peter, how can I explain it to you so that you will understand? In times to come, you will need to explain to others the importance of forgiveness, of love, so that you can lead others to My heart.

"If you had two donkeys, and they were needed to pull your cart a long way, you would try to treat them well, so that your destination would be reached. If one donkey became difficult, you would try all you could to persuade him to behave and to continue the journey. No matter how hard it was, you would keep trying in the hope that the donkey would respond to your requests. Even if the donkey did not, you would not undo his harness and chase him away, because he is valuable to you.

"It is the same with mankind. Some are difficult to guide...to help, but it does not mean you abandon them. Each person is valuable to God, and so it is your duty to try as hard as you can to bring each one into God's love. When it becomes difficult, see yourself as the good donkey, who, because he loves his companion, tries to pull the cart for him, in the hope that his companion will come to see that he is wanted as well."

Peter walked over to Judas and said, "Let me help you with your bag. Maybe today I can carry it for you." Judas looked at Peter with disbelief and wonderment that Peter would do this. "Well, if you want to you may carry it, but be careful you do not damage anything." My friend Peter turned and smiled softly at Me. I could see the beauty in his heart.

J
e
J e s u s
u
s

Jesus ††† 2-11-96

Bartholomew, walking beside Me, wondered, "Rabbi, if the kingdom of God is for all men, why were the Jewish people chosen to do God's will?"

I answered, "When God looked upon His children, He saw that those who lived closest to His heart were the sons and daughters of Israel. Their love was true and their desire to serve God was strong. To save the weak in the world, the Father chose the strong, for the strong would bring God's truth into the world."

Bartholomew was still unsure, and so he asked, "Why, then, is it that the Pharisees, the Sadducees, the priests, and most of Israel believe that they are the only true sons of God? They believe that Heaven is for them alone and that gentiles are not worthy of God and will not see Heaven."

"My friend," I replied, "what you say is true. Many believe that Heaven is only for the Jewish people and for no others. They do not understand that the Father created all peoples from His love, and wants them all to return to His love in Heaven. Like a child of a wealthy man, he is showered with gifts and treasures. His life is joyful with no cares and no worries. When he walks along the road he does not see the poor, the hungry, the sick, and those in need. He closes his eyes to them, believing they are a nuisance which should be ignored or treated with contempt. He is different from them because he is rich. He must be special, or why else would he have so much?

"What he does not see is that he is given this wealth to help others, to save others, and that when he does this, his Father is so happy with him that he showers him with more gifts. It is in the giving that you receive.

"What happens is, the son closes his heart to the needs of others, and just sees his own needs, his own comforts, his own desires. He becomes a selfish soul. His father one day looks upon his son and does not know him. His father sees selfishness and greed, and in despair takes his gifts from his son. The Father then shares them with those in need, and the son becomes the lost one, the beggar, and he wonders why this has happened.

"Over time, he comes to understand how wrong he was to close his heart to others. He then sees why he was given so much. It was to share with his brothers and sisters, not for himself alone. Now those who have the gifts and treasures of the Father, come to the son and offer him help. He sees now that the weak have become truly strong in the love of the Father, and in that strength they share willingly with all in need."

Bartholomew, looking at Me with understanding in his eyes, said, "Master, Your wisdom is so deep it touches my very soul. I see Israel is the spoiled son that will be shaken from slumber to understand all mankind are God's children, and that Heaven is for all." We walked in silence for awhile. Bartholomew then went off to discuss what I said with the others.

In the distance we could see a lake. Upon it were boats with fishermen casting their nets. As we came closer I could see in My follower's eyes their longing to fish again, for fishing was in their hearts.

Walking along the shore, we waded in the water feeling the coolness on our feet. Peter, James, and John came over to Me, and Peter spoke saying, "Master, it is so beautiful here. Maybe we could stay awhile and enjoy a little fishing."

"My friends, of course we can stay here. Yes, it is beautiful. Let us rest here for awhile."

Running into the water they began to splash each other, and diving into the water they were swimming about. Within moments everyone joined in, splashing, playing, relaxing, and enjoying themselves. Later, as they quieted down, some went off to fish while others made a fire and set to making a more comfortable area.

It was good to see them at ease. We had walked so far and done so much for My Father's glory, it was time to rest. Thomas was by My side remarking that he looked forward to eating fresh fish. "Lord," he said, "it will be good to eat fresh fish. The fish here are very tasty, I hope they catch plenty."

"Thomas, there will be enough for all. You will eat your fill and still there will be enough to feed all My followers." With a shout of delight, James came running along the shore with many fish in his arms, saying, "Lord, look at all we have caught!"

Thomas turned to Me and said, "We will eat well today." I looked into his eyes and could see the delight, the joy of the meal ahead. "Thomas, give thanks and praise to the Father, Who, in His mercy, sends you the food to sustain life." The disciples gathered together and I blessed the fish, thanking My Father for His generosity.

While the fish were cooking, the smell filled the air. Judas (not Iscariot) sat staring at the fish fascinated by the size of what had been caught. "Lord, the fish are so big. Never have I seen such fish. They smell wonderful, I am sure that they will taste good." His eyes grew larger thinking of the meal ahead.

"Look at the meal before you," I said to all My disciples. "The Father gives you all you need to do His work. He gives you what is needed, and more."

"Praise God!" shouted Thomas, and we began to praise and thank the Father. While we ate, the conversations were light...full of love and happiness.

13.

As the tasty meal settled in our stomachs, I explained, "Today you have eaten a wonderful meal with Me, a meal sent by the Father; but I tell you, in the future the meal the Father will offer you, will be the food of true life. The Father, through His Son, will offer you eternal sustenance...eternal life. The Father will offer you the true bread of life and the wine of forgiveness. I am the Son come down from Heaven, and I am the Bread that will fill your souls. I am the Wine that brings forgiveness. It is only through Me, His Son, that the Father offers the meal that gives eternal life. I am the Son, I am the food that the Father offers, I am the food that feeds your soul and fills you with the spirit of peace. Eat of Me and never hunger."

They looked uncertain, confused, so I said, "Eat and enjoy while you can, so that in times of need you will never hunger." They did not understand Me. "In times ahead you will look back and come to understand My meaning, and it will be for you to tell others."

"Lord, how can we ever understand? It is so difficult at times." It was Matthew speaking.

"Trust in My word. I tell you, after I return to My Father, you will be filled with wisdom from God, and all My words will come alive in your hearts."

Philip said, "If You say it is so, then it will be." After this we all slept.

It was late in the afternoon when we decided to go to the market in the next town, only a short distance away. When we arrived at the market there was a loud argument taking place. Two men were holding a woman between them shouting loudly. "She is a thief, she stole from my goods, she did not pay," said one.

The other was shouting, "I saw her steal. I saw her do it." The first man shouted, "Where is the magistrate? She must be punished." The crowd screamed over and over, "Thief, thief, thief!"

The poor woman, so thin, frail, and old, looked around in fear. She begged, "Have mercy. Have mercy on an old woman."

I stepped forward and took the woman's arms freeing her from the two men.

"What are you doing? She is a thief, she stole from me!" one man barked at Me.

"My friend, what did this woman steal that was so valuable?"

"She stole some grain; it is worth half a shekel," he said.

"Judas, pay this man one shekel for his grain." Judas looked shocked but he put his hand into his pocket and gave the man a shekel. The man cried, "But she stole. She sinned!" as he pointed an accusing finger at the old woman.

"Old woman, why did you steal?" I asked.

"Master, I stole because I have no food. My son died one year ago, and I have no one to support me. I asked my brothers and sisters here before you now to help me a little, but they refused. The tax collector took my home, the neighbors took my animals, and I have nothing left. Even the priests refuse to let me on the temple grounds, as I have no offerings to give to God except my prayers and my love."

She started to cry and fell at My feet saying, "Master, today You have shown me the first kindness since my son died. I will never forget You."

I looked around as those in the market stood in silence, looking at the ground in shame. "I tell you here today, not one of you has lived as your father Abraham asked. Not one of you has followed the commandments God gave to Moses. Not one of you has shown the mercy, the kindness, and the forgiveness each of you would expect for yourselves. As for your priests and elders, they bring shame upon themselves for treating a sister of theirs, a daughter of God, in such a way. The priests and elders only think of themselves, only think of wealth and fame. Those in need are ignored by those who should help them. No wonder the day is coming when a new church will arise, a church that truly is the temple of God. Shame on you all."

With that I left the people in silence and instructed My disciples to take the old woman to Elizabeth in Judea, who would care for her as if she were her own.

15.

J
e
J e s u s
u
s

Jesus ††† 2-12-96

Leaving the village, we passed the synagogue and many were gathered outside. A group of Pharisees came forward. "Just a moment. You there, Who are you?" said one.

"I am Jesus of Nazareth," I replied. There was silence for a moment as they stood looking at Me. One, mockingly, spoke out, "So this is the great prophet. Tell us something so that we may learn."

"There are those who will never learn, for they close their hearts to God's will. It has been written by the prophets to treat all with kindness and respect, but how many here listen? The Father in Heaven has given commandments of love, but how many listen? I look into your hearts and see you counting your coins, amassing a fortune, and not considering others. Do you really believe this is what God wants from you? I see you full of greed and jealousy. Is this how God hoped you would be? Look into your own heart and see the sins you commit; see them for what they are. Do not let your pride hide your sins."

Taken aback, the man stuttered a reply, "How can you see in my heart? How is it possible you know me?"

I replied, "I have known you from the day you were born. I was with you when you stole your brother's cloak and sold it so you could have money to buy your pleasures."

He fell to his knees trembling. "Master, forgive me. No one knew that, but You do! Forgive me, and I will change." Looking upon him I leaned down and took his arm, helping him to his feet. He was like so many others lost along the way.

"Change your life from today. Spend your life praising God and helping others. You will find your forgiveness there. Just accept it and live a life of goodness, not greed." All those around looked away in fear that I would look into their hearts and see their true selves. We returned to the lake. When we arrived, we prayed to the Father that He would soften men's hearts and forgive their sins.

The evening drew on. It was very dark, with only the light of the fire to keep the darkness away. I looked at the embers floating up in the heat...oh, so bright at first, but then fading and dying. They reminded Me of mankind. So many profess their love of God, but as time goes on, the love seems to fade away replaced by self importance and self first; then they just disappear into the dark.

A slow mournful song was being sung by Andrew; it came from his heart. The others began to clap slowly and join in the song. Andrew was singing about a love betrayed for money...how a young man was paid by a wealthy man to leave his daughter, whom the young man had been seeing and hoping to marry. When the daughter discovered her love had taken money instead of her, it broke her heart. She could not eat, and so she died. It reminded Me again how many reject the love of God for wealth and fame in the world. A sad song and a sad world.

I awoke with My Father's voice filling My heart. I arose and walked to a secluded spot where I could be alone with Him. I sat there for some hours speaking with My Father, discussing what He asked of Me and how I should fulfill it. Each time I thought of what would be, I wondered at how mankind had been led away so easily, and of the payment I would have to give to redeem them.

There was a battle with My human self which feared what was ahead, and My Divine Self which longed to forgive mankind. The evil one was always in the shadows trying to fill Me with fear and anxiety, but I ignored his vain attempts. The Father strengthened Me with His love, encouraged Me with His words, and lifted Me into His heart. United in the Father, nothing was impossible, nothing was to be denied, and nothing could stop Me.

My Father's love...so powerful, so soft, so strengthening, and so welcoming. I knew I must give My life, so that all of My children, My family on earth, could share this eternal bliss. United with My Father, the Holy Spirit became one with Me, and together We shared Our love.

17.

J
E
J E S U S
U
S

Jesus ††† 2-14-96

I walked back to My followers where they were cooking a light meal of fish. It was already the middle of the day. When I arrived back, Thomas said, "Master, You have been gone a long time. We were concerned."

"There is no need to worry, Thomas, I was with My Father." Simon (not Simon Peter) came forward offering Me some fish which I took, and for which I thanked My Father.

Simon said in a very quiet voice, "They have been arguing again, Master." I looked and saw Judas sitting by himself with his back to the others while Peter, John, and James looked at the ground in embarrassment. "What have you disagreed about this time?" I asked.

Peter looked up and said, "Judas said we should go to the larger towns so we can make money for our work. We said that we should go where You want."

"It is more than that," wailed Judas, "they say I am only here with You to make money; they say I only love money. Master, it is true I worry over how we will eat, how we will buy clothes, how we will pay for shelter, but it is necessary to do so or we cannot survive. We never have much, we usually live day to day relying on good will to feed us. All I say is let us take collections, just what the people can afford, so that we can live a little more comfortably."

"Judas, do not worry so much, trust in My Father. Can you not see how He has provided for us already? Can you not see it is better to have a little, given in love, than a lot, given as a duty? We do not need more than we are given, we do not need collections, we only need to trust and all will be provided. If we look to make profit, then we are no better than the Pharisees. We must look to the souls that are saved. That is the true reward. I can understand your concern, My friend, for you worry about our well being, but learn to trust in Me a little more and find peace.

"As for you, My brothers, do not argue with such deep feelings. It is better to discuss in a civil, loving way your disagreements, so that you can find the answers without anyone being offended. What good is it to win an argument, if you lose a friend?" They looked at each other a little red-faced and then started to pack their belongings, getting ready to leave for the next town.

J
E
J E S U S
U
S

Jesus ††† 2-19-96

The wind blew dust into our faces as we walked the path to the village. A storm was coming. You could feel it in the air. The atmosphere was oppressive and the sky was dark. It started to rain, lightly at first, and then a downpour with thunder and lightning. We ran for cover in a little hut that was in poor condition. It was used to store bits and pieces needed to maintain the vineyard that we had entered.

"How long do you think the rain will last?" asked Philip, to no one in particular.

Judas said, "With our luck we will be stranded here for days."

Peter looked at Me and smiled softly, then said, "My friends, let us make the best of it. Let us pray to God our Father. Let us celebrate our love of God together. Let us praise His Holy Name, then this time will be a joyful time."

"Well said, Peter," I responded, and as we all knelt, I began to pray, "Father, we Your children who love You completely, come to You in prayer...come to praise You for Your wonderful gift of love to us. Father, I come before You as Your Son. I come to ask that Your favor shine upon My followers, who have so much to do in their lives for Your glory. I ask, when the time is right, that You fill them with the strength they need to do Your will." Together then we praised the Father for His mercy.

A little later the rain stopped and we started out for the town again. There was a sweet, clean smell in the air...a feeling of freshness. Everyone walked with joy in their steps, joy that had come from prayer, and now was magnified by the coolness in the air. "Master, isn't it wonderful how the rain cleanses and seems to renew the land?" said James.

"Yes, My child, it is. Think of the rain as the forgiving mercy of God, and when it falls upon a soul it wipes away the stain of sin and renews the person's heart. A divine gift that will be given to all the children of God with the sacrifice of the Lamb of forgiveness... a divine mercy that will be offered to all...a divine offering that only needs to be accepted, to be received."

J
E
J E S U S
U
S

Jesus ††† 2-20-96

The sound of horses and men marching quickly could be heard and then a garrison of Roman soldiers passed us heading for the village. The clatter of their weapons and the stamping of their feet almost deafened us as they passed.

When we arrived at the village it was in turmoil. The soldiers had searched the houses for rebels and had arrested five men whom they were treating harshly. The villagers were gathered around begging the Romans to free the men. They proclaimed the innocence of the men and called for their release. The Centurion on his horse would not listen and ordered his soldiers to push the crowd back.

As they did, a young boy broke free and ran forward crying, "Father, father." A large burly soldier hit the child very hard with his closed fist and the young boy, who was about four years old, fell to the ground and began to convulse. The crowd became silent as the officer boomed to the soldier, "You fool, he is only a child!"

The officer jumped from his horse and leaned over the child who had stopped convulsing and was now dead. As he removed his helmet, tears were seen running down his face and he cried, "He is only a child, a baby. My son is this age, a baby." He began to sob from his heart.

I walked forward as the crowd parted to make way for Me. The soldiers looked as if to stop Me when someone shouted, "It is Jesus of Nazareth, the great prophet, the great healer." Hearing this, the soldiers stood back and I went to the child. The Centurion looked at Me and said, "Can You help?" In his heart I could see a lost soul, one full of the pain of the work he did, full of death and destruction...but hidden behind this confusion, I could also see compassion, love, and hope.

"I will," was My reply as I leaned forward and picked up the child. "But he is dead," said the soldier who had hit the boy. "There is nothing You can do now." I gave him a soft smile and said, "My Father, Who sent Me, gives or takes life. It is His to command...and if it is His will that this child lives, then he will live."

"Then Your Father must be a magician," said the soldier. "No, My Father is the God of Creation Who made all things and it *is* His will that this child lives." As I said this, the child awoke crying, "Mother!"

The soldier stood back amazed as the child's mother came and took him...full of joy, full of thanks and praising God for His mercy. The soldiers were still staring at Me as the crowd began to praise God in unison. "Who are You?" shouted a soldier in fear. "I Am," I said, and the crowd became silent. "What sort of an answer is that? I asked who You are, and You say, 'I Am.'"

"I am the Son, I am the Lamb, and I am the forgiveness of God." The Centurion jumped on his horse nervously and snapped at his men, "Set those prisoners free. We do not want them." He looked at Me and gave a nod of thanks as he rode off leading his men from the village.

J
E
J E S U S
U
S

Jesus ††† 2-25-96

The villagers came to Me asking Me to touch them, to heal them, and to speak to them. I stood among them and said, "You saw how the Father in Heaven, through His Son, touched the child today and brought life to his body. The Father wants to touch all of His children and bring them to life...life in His love."

A man came forward and said, "My house is Your house. Please come and eat with me." As we walked to his house, the crowd followed. "You cannot all come," he cried, "there is not enough room." I turned to them, and said, "Today I will rest, and tomorrow I will come to you in the market place."

"Master, Master, if You just say the word, I will be healed," called out a blind man. "Your faith has healed you," I said.

"I can see, I can see!" he shouted, "Praise God, praise the Lord, I can see. I can see!" He came to Me and took My hand and kissed it saying, "Master, You are the Lord, and I thank You for Your mercy. Praise God!"

"My friend, God has healed you, always remember that. Every day remember what the Father has done for you through His Son, and thank God for His love."

We entered the courtyard of the house, and a large man rushed forward to the master of the house. "Master," he said, "we cannot feed the whole village." "Set places for my visitors, and then give what you can to those in need, not those whom we know have plenty, but to the poor and the beggars, for today God has shown His love, and today I will share my food in thanks for God's mercy."

I looked at the owner of the house and saw into his heart, a heart that loved God, and a heart that today had learned to share. This was the true miracle of today.

J
E
J E S U S
U
S

Jesus ††† 2-26-96

The next day as I walked with My disciples to the market place, children were following Me and running forward to hold My hand. "Don't bother the Master. Be off with you," shouted one of My followers.

"Let the children come to Me. Do not chase them away. Their love is pure and it brings Me great joy." As I said this all the children crowded around Me, happy and smiling. I looked into their hearts and felt happy. How I wanted all mankind to be as they are.

One child would not let go of My hand. He just held on and looked up at Me with big brown eyes. "My child, your grip is so strong you may hurt My hand," I said in humor. He said nothing but just kept holding on and kept looking at Me. I leaned down and picked him up saying, "What is your name, child?" He looked at Me and said, shyly, "John."

"John is a good name. It is the name of a true friend of God," I said. "I love God," replied the boy. "God loves you also, and watches over you because He cares for you," I said.

He asked, "Does God listen to my prayers? My mother and father say He does."

"My child, every prayer you say is taken into God's heart. The Father in Heaven waits to hear every word of love you offer Him when you pray," I answered, smiling at the boy.

"You are a nice man, I like You. Please stay in our village and do not leave us," he pleaded as children do. "I must leave soon as there are others who need Me, but know that I will always be with you. I promise you that every moment of your life, I will be with you in love, and My angels will watch over you until you meet Me with My Father in Heaven."

I looked into his eyes and saw the tears forming as he was about to cry. I kissed him on the cheek and said, "You must be strong for you will bring others to Me. You will be My friend forever, and, as a friend, you must show how much you love Me with a strong heart and a strong faith."

"I will," he sobbed. "I will, because You are my friend." He rubbed the tears from his eyes as he heard his mother call, "John Mark, where are you?"

J
e
J e s u s
u
s

Jesus ††† 3-2-96

At the market place a large number of people had gathered, and as they saw Me walk towards them, they rushed forward shouting, "It is the prophet, Jesus." When My disciples had quieted them and asked them to sit, I spoke to them saying, "It takes a miracle for many to believe in God, and yet every day God's miracles are before you. It is just that, often, they go unnoticed. The air you breathe is one of God's miracles, but how many give it a second thought? The water you drink, the food you eat...miracles of God, but how many think of this? When you look upon each other, created in God's likeness, a miracle...but how many see? So many miracles before you each moment of your lives, and yet you look for more! Understand what you have from God with every moment of your life, and see God's miracles in everything."

"Rabbi," called a young man, "the air is always here, the food is grown by man's efforts, the water comes from the mountains. Each of us comes from our mother's womb. We know where these things come from, we know God created all things and then gave it to man to use for his needs. We know that life in the womb came from God, but through man and woman. We know the plants we eat are there by God's will, and that, with our joining in God's creation to cultivate the crops, we have our food. We know God gave us the water, and when we use it wisely, it is clean to drink and water for our crops. We know these things, Rabbi. What we do not know is how You raised the dead to life...how you heal the sick. Tell us so we can understand what You do, and in the understanding, develop it for our benefit, as we have with all the other gifts God has given us!"

I looked at him and felt sadly, sad at the selfishness and pride within. "If you know these things, if you know of God's miracles, why do you not believe and follow what God has commanded. If you truly knew what God gives you with every moment of your life, you would spend eternity thanking and praising God. If you understood what God gives you with all of creation, you would not squander it, you would not waste. Instead, you would share it with your brothers and sisters.

"It is a prideful generation who says they know God's creation, and that they are masters of it. It is a selfish generation which thinks God's gifts are for them, and them alone. It is a sinful generation that ignores what God offers, or sees it as mankind's just rewards. It is a greedy generation that undervalues what it has and then asks for more. It is no wonder God is unhappy when His children act so. Look within yourselves and see how you are, and then try to see how offensive to God you must be. When you have done this, ask for forgiveness and the grace to change your lives to become true children of the Father. You will see then, the miracle of God's great mercy."

The crowd was silent, all looking at the young man, who was now red with embarrassment. "I am sorry, Rabbi, to offend You. I have so much to learn. Maybe You could teach me," he said.

"My friend, today you have learned a great lesson, the lesson of humility. I know your heart is true because of your humble acceptance of My words. If only all mankind could be this way, then the love of God would reign in all men's hearts."

The people came forward bringing the sick to be healed. The young man sat at the side watching. After the crowd left, he came to Me and said, "Can

I follow you?" I replied, "My road is a hard road to travel, and there are so many difficulties that many give up, because they are not strong enough to carry on."

"I would be, Rabbi," was his answer.

"Go back to your family for they need you. Your father is old and he relies on you," I said.

"Rabbi, how will I learn then?" he quizzed, looking sad.

I reached out and put My hand on his shoulder. "Learn from Holy Scripture. See the Word of God and find all you need there. It will teach you how God wants you to live. Then live your life as a gift to God, not only taking from God. Do this and you will find the knowledge you seek, and then one day I will see you again in your new life to come."

After we had talked a little longer, he left to return to his family, and I felt a little sad. Here was a man who, like many, thought that he knew God and God's wishes, but now he had been touched by the truth, and he understood that he knew little at all.

J
E
J E S U S
U
S

Jesus ††† 3-4-96

We left the village and headed for Capernaum. The day was drawing to a close and it was time to leave. Judas spoke up, "Master, shouldn't we stay in the village another night, as we will have comfortable beds to sleep in?" The others looked at Me in agreement with him.

"My friends, wherever we sleep tonight we will find comfort, for we will sleep in My Father's hands," I said, as I continued to lead them from the village. "Let's sing a song of praise to the Father," I said happily, longing to lead them in the worship of God. The words danced from their mouths as they sang joyfully of God's glory and, as the words united in praise of the Father, their hearts were opened to God's love.

After we finished singing, it began to get dark and in the distance we saw a solitary light.

"Master, let us go there and see if we can find shelter there," cried Peter. We headed towards the light and as we drew nearer, we could see a solitary figure within a small house. In his hands he was holding the Holy Scripture and singing psalms to God.

Peter said, "It is a holy man, let us ask for his help."

"Peter, my friend, it is he who needs our help." He looked confused, so I said, "Look and see."

As we came closer, My disciples began to see that this man was a leper. That was why he was by himself away from the village. "Master," shouted Judas (not Iscariot), "we should keep away from him lest we become sick."

"Judas, if you see a sick man, you are to help, not turn away from him. Have you learned nothing yet?" I said. "But, Master," stuttered Thomas, "we may become as he."

In reply I said, "Thomas, and all of you, do you not yet know that I am here to heal the sick, to set sinners free, and to bring God's love to all. Have you seen so much and still do not understand? I will heal this man, and he will have his burden lifted from him, but will you keep the burden of self on your souls? **To trust in God means to give yourself completely without concern to what may happen.** If you give because of your love for God, then God will protect you; do you not believe this?"

They looked at each other, uncertain, until Peter stepped forth and said, "Let us go to our brother and offer him our help." The others murmured awhile, then John said, "The Master always shows love and always helps. Why do we wonder now and try to stop Him? I am with Peter."

"So am I," said James, and soon we were all walking towards the house in prayer to the Father.

Simon knocked on the door, and the praying within the house stopped. There was a shuffling towards the door. The door opened and the man appeared in the doorway, his face terribly scarred from the disease.

"This is a leper's house, my friends, it is best you keep away." Simon stepped back in shock at seeing the deformed face. Then in the true love that he had within, Simon said, "We know you are a leper, and we have come to help you. Our Master wishes to see you and talk with you."

"You are welcome, but I must not let you in, or you will share in my suffering. It is enough that I suffer, but I do not wish to give my sufferings to you also. Please go, before it is too late. Please go, my friends," he pleaded.

I stepped forward into the light saying, "It does not matter how you appear. You are a beautiful man with a loving heart. You pray to My Father in Heaven each day, not for yourself, but for others. This is the true love that all men should have." He looked surprised and said, "How did you know that?"

"The Father and the Son are one. What the Father knows, the Son knows, and prayers to the Father are prayers to the Son." He was confused, and so I put My hand on his shoulder as he tried to step back.

"You will get my disease, please don't touch me. I could not stand it if I caused another to suffer." His voice trembled as he spoke. "My Father hears your prayers and sends His Son to heal you," I said, and leaned forward to kiss his forehead. "Be healed by the true love of God you have within."

"Master," shouted James, "his face, his face!"

The others started to call out as well, "His sores have gone."

"He is healed, praise God!"

The man touched his face and looked at his hands, as tears rolled down his cheeks. "It is gone, it is gone," he cried. He tore his clothes off to look at his body; it was clean and perfect in every way. Sobbing he fell to his knees. "Thank You, Master, thank You. I thank God in Heaven for His mercy. Thank You, thank You."

I took his hand and helped him to his feet. "God looks after His children, and your trust in Him makes you a true child of God. Let us kneel down and pray to the Father in thanks," I said.

After prayers, the man invited us to eat with him, and he served us a wonderful meal which filled

My followers' stomachs and made them happy. "What was in that delicious food?" asked Bartholomew.

"Some larks, and some fish from the lake," the man answered.

"But it tasted so good, there surely must have been something else in it?" queried Bartholomew.

"It is the joy of God's mercy that you saw tonight, which makes the meal sweeter," I cut in. "When you see God's love in action and feel its touch, all becomes sweet."

The discussion went on into the night, with the leper so full of God's spirit and God's joy, that he could not sleep. Finally I laid My hand upon him and said, "Rest now, for tomorrow you have your whole life before you, whole in God." He fell asleep looking so happy and so peaceful. James crept quietly to Me saying, "Master, I am glad we came here." He put his head on My shoulder and slept soundly.

J
E
J E S U S
U
S

Jesus ††† 3-6-96

In the early hours of the morning, I awoke and moved James from My shoulder. His face was angelic as he slept. Quietly I walked to the door and stepped outside. The air was fresh and cool and it was still dark. I walked along a path and prayed to My Father in Heaven.

As I prayed, My body felt renewed, full of energy, and full of the Father's love. I asked My Father for guidance, and before Me in a vision, I saw the gates of the temple in Jerusalem. They were closed and chained. My Father said, "The temple is closed, not only to many of My children, but it is also closed to Me. Open the gates and rebuild the temple with Your love as the foundation."

"Father, the gates will be unlocked and mankind's hearts opened to Your love, so that Our family of man can enjoy eternal life in Heaven," I replied.

29.

"My Son, the sacrifice You must make is a necessity to defeat evil. You must carry the sins of mankind and surround them with Your love. It is Your love of Our children that will bring them redemption."

"Father, at times I wonder if I will have the strength to do as You ask but then I know I must, so that Our children can be free." Later I returned to the house where breakfast was being prepared, and in My heart I was still thinking of what was to come.

"Master, You look so sad." It was John speaking. He often was the first to notice My return.

"It is nothing, My friend. I was just thinking of the road ahead," I replied.

"If it is too far for You to walk today, we can rest here longer," was John's concerned reply.

"The road I must walk, is a road I must walk alone," I said.

Not understanding, John said, "I will walk with You to the end of the world if You would ask me."

He had a hurt look on his face, so I said, "John, My dear John, you will walk a long way for Me and I will always be at your side, even though you may not know it. The path I talk of, is the path that shows the Way, and many will follow it in their search for their true home."

"Master, You confuse me at times, for when You talk I can make little sense of it," stated John.

"Let's eat," I said. "We can talk later, and in time you will come to understand."

J
E
J E S U S
U
S

Jesus †‡† 3-9-96

We entered Capernaum which was full of people, so busy buying and selling, so busy enjoying themselves, **so busy that they often forgot God**. My followers and I headed for the synagogue to offer prayers to the Father. All around us people were haggling, signing contracts, eating, and drinking. Capernaum...a hub of activity, a joining of the roads... a place to where many were drawn.

The synagogue was nearly empty, with only a few older men praying and reading Scripture. Some of them turned to look at us as we entered, then carried on with their prayers. I sat down and closed My eyes thinking of My Father. Outside the synagogue noise filled the air, but inside it was quiet. My disciples began to pray, and I felt love and trust in each word. We stayed there for some hours before leaving to find a place to sleep.

Judas Iscariot went to find rooms and took Andrew with him. While we waited, I said to My disciples, "I want to tell you about a man who rushed every day, except the Sabbath. Even on the Sabbath he wanted to do so much. With great restraint he stopped himself for he knew this day was holy...an offering to God. His neighbors made fun of him for the way he behaved.

"Now his neighbors did not rush at all. They took everything at a slow pace, and when the Sabbath came, they only pretended to worship the Lord. If they could do something else without others finding out, they would. The man who rushed, worked hard, provided for his family, and paid his tithes. While the others provided for their families, they often avoided their tithes. The man who rushed could find time in his busy life for God, yet those who had so much time to waste, could only give God the time that was forced upon them.

"When the man who rushed died, Abraham stood before him and said, 'Your life has been so busy, but even so, you showed your love and respect for God. You are welcome in Heaven.'

"When the neighbors died, Abraham said, 'Your lives have been full of sin, wasting the valuable time God gave you. You showed little respect for God or fellow man, living lives full of greed and full of self. How can you expect to be welcomed in Heaven?'

"The neighbors said, 'We did not want to kill ourselves rushing to and fro, but we did celebrate the Sabbath, except when there were good reasons not to do so.'

"Abraham replied, 'You deceitful men, you even deceive yourselves. When is there a good reason to avoid praising God on the one day that you are asked to do so? If you had been busy in your lives it would have been to your advantage to rest with God on the Sabbath, for He would have given you the strength you needed to carry on. Look at the man you made fun of. He was always busy but he kept the Sabbath for God. He showed how, even with a full life, one can still spend time with God. You, with an empty life, nevertheless, had no time for God.'

"Abraham closed the gate of Heaven to these men and sent them to hell for eternity. Do you understand what I am saying to you?"

James spoke up, "Yes, Lord, no matter how hard you work always make time for God."

"Yes, James, that is part of it," I said.

Bartholomew said, "Lord, it shows you must not waste your life being lazy, and that you must keep the Sabbath holy."

"Well said, Bartholomew, but there is something else," I replied. They looked at each other and could not see anything other than what they had said. "It is this...life is a gift from God, and to be lazy or to waste your life is a rejection of God's gift. Often people try to avoid their responsibilities, they shirk their duties and let others do it. They believe that if they can get away with it without anyone knowing, then it is not wrong.

"What they forget is that God knows, and when you face your Creator, He will know what you have done with the gift He gave you. If you have wasted it, He will not reward you, but if you have lived a life that bears fruit, fruit for God, then you will be rewarded with eternal life. Remember, when God gives you a gift, it is to be used, not wasted."

Judas and Andrew returned. They found shelter for us with a follower of Mine. "Lord," cried Judas, "Simon lives here. You remember Simon, whose mother you cured? He welcomes us in his house, and he will not take a penny," he said gleefully.

"It is true, Lord. Simon asks You to come to his house, where he is at this moment, preparing a meal for You," said Andrew, looking at Judas with disappointment in his face. I could see how hurt Andrew was, and so I took him to one side and asked, "What is wrong?"

"Nothing, Master," he replied, looking to the ground.

"It is not good to lie, even to protect another, for it is still a sin. Come, My friend, tell Me."

"Lord, it is Judas. He went to Simon and demanded he let You stay there. He demanded, and he should not have. Anyway, Simon wanted You to stay with him, regardless of what Judas said."

I responded, "It is difficult at times for Judas for he expects so much. He does not understand that all you need, you will find in Me."

"Lord, when You see Simon please tell him that it was not my wish to ask him for money," Andrew whispered.

"How much did Judas take?" I said.

"Twenty silver coins."

"So much money. What did he want it for?" I replied.

"Judas said it was to help You, Lord," Andrew responded.

"Leave it to Me, Andrew, and do not worry any more. I know your heart is true."

We arrived at Simon's house, and he ran to welcome Me. "Master, I am so happy You are here," he said, kissing My hand.

"Dear Simon, you are so kind to welcome us into your home, and I see you have prepared a banquet for us," I remarked.

"It is the least I can do for my Lord," Simon said, in humility.

"Judas," I said, turning to look at him, "give Simon 25 pieces of silver for all the trouble he has gone to, and for welcoming us into his house."

"But-but-but, Master," spluttered Judas, "it would only cost a fraction of that to stay at an inn."

"What is money among friends? We do not need it, for the Father sends so many good people to help," I said, smiling at Judas.

"I-I-I," stuttered Judas, as Andrew took the money bag, and said, "let me help you." Andrew then gave the coins to Simon while Judas looked amazed. I said, looking at Judas, "Money is not important, it is the souls of men I take to the Father; this is the true treasure of life. If anyone loves money more than his brothers and sisters, then the doors to Heaven will be closed to him." I turned and walked to the table and the beautiful meal awaiting us.

J
e
J e s u s
u
s

Jesus ††† 3-10-96

After the meal, we sat together discussing the events of the past few days. James said, "Lord, I enjoyed so much the time at the lake...the fish were delicious, and there were so many."

"No, I think the best time was at the leper's house," said Philip. I could see in Philip's heart, the joy he had from the cure of this dear man.

Peter spoke, "Every moment in some way has been special, be it healing the leper, eating the fish, praying in the temple, bringing the child to life, or filling the people with God's word...every moment a joy and from every moment, something to learn."

I knew Peter spoke from his heart and truly meant what he said. Peter, My trusted friend, did not know yet that he had been given a special gift to help him guide My children when I return to the Father.

"I think every moment is special, like Peter, but to me the thanks of the villagers and the gifts they gave us, warms my heart," said Judas. Everyone looked at him, some with disbelief but others with pity.

"Judas, you must start to think more with your heart, rather than your pocket," said Thomas.

"My heart is open to those in need," defended Judas. "Why else do you think I would walk this hard road with you?" With puzzled looks on their faces most were wondering why, indeed, he was with us.

"Judas," I said, "my dear friend, try to think a little less of material things and more about your soul. I know it is hard at times, especially when you are cold or hungry. Then material wealth can seem so important. Look at those rich men who have so much. See how they worry about what to do with their wealth...how not to lose it, how they can have more, how they wonder if their friends are only friends because of their wealth.

"They have a life of worry, but then, like everyone else, they die. All the wealth in the world cannot prevent death. In death they find they cannot take the riches of this world with them, but they can take only the treasures of the spirit. In death the true value of material things is seen...it is of little value at all... maybe a fine coffin and a large sepulcher, but what are they if you do not have the richness of the spirit that takes you to the Father in Heaven?"

Judas looked around him and seemed to shrink in size. Once again he was hurt, he was feeling as if we were all against him; he was feeling so sorry for himself.

Peter slapped Judas on the back and embraced him saying, "It's not that bad, my friend, we are all learning...so don't be so hard on yourself."

Judas looked at him and gave a weak smile saying, "Thank you, I am glad you understand."

J
E
J E S U S
U
S

Jesus ††† 3-13-96

We lay down to sleep and Matthew lay next to Me. "Master, when we sleep and sometimes have bad dreams, or dreams of doing wrong, is it a sin?" he asked.

"Matthew, you can expect when you are most vulnerable, the evil one will try to confuse you. Sometimes for those who are close to God, the only time he can play his tricks is when you are asleep. If you reject in your sleep, what you reject when you are awake, then it is not a sin. It is when you welcome these dreams of evil, of lust, of greed, that you sin," I replied.

"But Lord, they seem to be there often, and when I wake, I feel so disappointed in myself for allowing them to happen," whispered Matthew.

I responded, "My friend, the fact you feel this way shows that you do not welcome them, and that you do reject them. It is not your fault if he puts these thoughts in your mind, but it is your love of God that helps you to reject them. Do not be so worried. As long as you reject these thoughts, you do not sin."

Matthew was a lot happier now, for he had serious concerns that he was at fault. He understood that evil placed in front of you does not make you a sinner; it is the acceptance of it that does. He closed his eyes and slept soundly.

J
e
J e s u s
u
s

Jesus ††† 3-16-96

The next morning it was raining quite heavily. As we stood looking out of the window, Thomas said, "I don't think we will be going anywhere today."

My heart was full of the Father, and I longed to go to the synagogue to pray and to read Scripture. I said, "The synagogue is not far. Let us go there for awhile."

"But you will get soaked," said our host.

"A little rain will do no harm," I replied, as I walked out of the door. The others followed and the rain stopped suddenly.

"How can this be?" said Peter, "It was pouring down rain a second ago." I turned and smiled at him, and he understood, without a word being said.

We entered the synagogue and began to read Scripture. I was reading the passages about Jonah and the people of Nineveh, when someone stood up and said, "Look, it is Jesus, the Nazarene." Those in the temple turned to look at me, and waited expectantly for Me to speak.

"My brothers, today I am thinking about Jonah, and how he went to Nineveh and asked the people to change. With God in their hearts, the Ninevites repented and asked for God's forgiveness and God's love. To understand this part of Holy Scripture would bring many to see the lesson for those of this generation. God sends His love asking for repentance and offering forgiveness, but unlike the Ninevites, who saw the truth in the word, this generation turns its back on God's offering...God's gift. This generation has closed its heart to God and only thinks of its own well being, its own position, and its own wealth. In this generation the Ninevites would only find shame!"

I sat down to silence. Then after a few moments thinking on what I had said, a Pharisee stood up. "How dare You!" he shouted. "How dare You accuse us of this. We pray. We spend time with God in the temple. How dare You!" As he sat down, he continued to glare at Me.

I remained silent as another spoke, "Who are You to condemn us? Who are You that You understand Scripture so much, while we who have studied Scripture for many years do not see in it what You do? Who taught You? Who was Your teacher, that You can speak that way?"

I did not reply, but just sat silently as My disciples fidgeted nervously. "Get out. Get out of the temple, you blasphemer. Get out, You are not welcome here!" shouted another.

The people in the temple were shouting more and more as I rose and said, "In the love of God, you would only show love, not hate. In the love of God you would listen and hear. In the love of God you would not deny what you know to be true. This generation condemns itself and this generation cannot see it."

Their protests got louder, and as a group they surrounded Me. Peter stood up and said, "Master, let us leave before they become violent."

With My disciples I returned to Simon's house to bid him farewell. After we spoke to Simon and were ready to leave, a commotion started outside the house.

It was the people from the synagogue, the priests, and the synagogue guards. They were calling for Me to come out to face them.

Simon said, "It is best that You leave quickly by the side door, or they will stone You."

"Thank you, My friend for your hospitality and thank you for your help," I said, as we left by the side entrance. As we left Capernaum we looked back and could see the crowd still outside Simon's house.

J
e
J e s u s
u
s

Jesus ††† 3-17-96

We walked for some hours, and as we walked we praised My Father in Heaven. I could feel the joy in the voices of My disciples, as their hearts were filled with the Father's love. Peter was walking by My side, when he turned and said, "Lord, that was very difficult in the synagogue. The people were very angry."

"Yes, Peter, they were," I said, "but it is often like that. When the truth is spoken, it is often denied and answered in anger."

"Lord, You must be more careful in what You say, and where You say it," said Peter.

"Peter, I am here to speak the truth, to stand against evil, and to show God's love to all. I am here to show the Way...and to show it may upset some, but it will save so many!"

Peter was quiet for a long time, and then he said, "If that is what You must do, I will be with You through it all."

"I know you will, My friend, but I also know in your humanity you will weaken at times, but then you will find your strength in Me and become a rock of true faith," I said.

Looking concerned, Peter said, "My Lord, I will never let You down."

"Peter, in all you do, I love you, and in all you do, I am with you, even when you weaken," I said, smiling softly at him as we continued to walk along the road.

J
e
J e s u s
u
s

Jesus ††† 3-21-96

It was getting late in the afternoon when Judas (not Iscariot) came up to Me and asked, "Master, we have done so much in the past months, why do You not rest more? When You are not teaching and healing, You walk with us from town to town. You must be so tired. I wonder how You do so much."

"Judas, My friend," I replied, "I am only with you for a little while, but while I am here, there is so much to do for the Father. I was sent to do this work, and so the Father will give Me all I need to fulfill His wishes. **In times to come, those who do My work will be given all they need to complete their tasks.** The Father, through His Son, will send the Holy Spirit to strengthen all who do God's work. The Holy Spirit will fill the hearts of God's chosen in abundance. They will have all the gifts required for what is asked of them."

"Is it the Holy Spirit that fills You, then, Master?" asked Judas.

"The Holy Spirit is one with Me, and I am one with the Father. All I do, I do for the Father, with the Holy Spirit, and of the Son," I said to Judas, who looked confused. "Judas, it is difficult to understand, I know, but know that I and the Father are one with the Spirit, and all the Spirit does, and will do, comes from the Father and from Me, His only Son."

Judas was thinking hard and then said, "Lord, I know You are the Messiah. I know the Father has sent You to bring us home to Him. I know You are the living love of God...but I just don't understand it!"

"Do not try, My friend. Just keep that faith in your heart and believe in Me," I said, putting My arm around his shoulder and embracing him. His faith filled My heart with joy. A simple, pure, innocent faith that all should have, but often deny with their constant search for answers that they can never have until they are in Heaven.

As evening drew on, we sat under a bridge and lit a fire. The coolness of the evening embraced us as we huddled closer to the fire. Matthew was preparing some bread and wine, mixed with water, for our supper. As he did so he prayed to the Father, "Yahweh, my Lord, my God, I ask You to fill our hearts with Your love, through the food we eat, food which is a gift from You."

At that moment, I saw the last time I would eat with My friends, and I saw the perpetual sacrifice offered around the world in so many churches and in so many hearts.

"Matthew, share the bread among us and come and sit next to Me," I said gently. He came and sat beside Me, and together we all thanked the Father for His gift of the meal. As we were eating I said to Matthew, "Tonight, with the bread, wine, and water you prepared, you became a vision of what is to come." Matthew looked puzzled, so I said, "Don't worry, My friend, Let's all pray together to the Father."

Lifting our voices after the meal, we praised the Father. I could see My disciples' hearts full of love, all except one, who was full of confusion. After praying, we slept soundly through the night leaning against each other to keep warm. Matthew was like a child in My arms, looking so peaceful in his sleep. With this vision before Me, I fell asleep.

J
e
J e s u s
u
s

Jesus ††† 3-24-96

We were awoken by shouts and screams. It was still dark. Climbing up to the road we saw two men beating another. Through the darkness we could see and hear the sticks pounding against his flesh, and now the man, lying on the ground, only groaned. As we approached the men, they looked at us, at first surprised, and then ready to fight.

"What are you doing? You will kill him!" shouted Peter, as he walked towards them.

"It is all he deserves," said the taller of the two men. "He left my house without paying his bill."

"And so you would kill him for that?" I said.

"Yes, he is a liar and a thief," replied the man. "He ate our food, he wore our clothes, and drank our wine. Then he sneaks out in the night without paying, as he promised to do. We cannot afford to give our food away freely, as we would have every beggar coming for help."

"Would it be so bad if they did?" I asked.

"We would be bankrupt!" shouted the man. "Be off with you and let us finish our business."

"What good will killing him do. It will not bring back your money," I said, as My disciples gathered around the man on the ground to protect him.

"So you would protect a thief, a sinner! That makes you no better than he," he said, raising his stick threateningly.

"Forgiveness is called for in Scripture. Love is called for by God, and mercy is offered to all by the Father," I said, gently.

"I am not interested in Scripture, and anyway, this man has stolen. This man has lied, and who knows what else he has done?"

With sadness in My heart I said, "If you kill this man you will have to pay the price, for God has commanded you, 'thou shalt not kill.'"

"Ah, yes, but God also says thou shalt not lie or steal," he replied, happy with himself.

"That is true, and the man who does these, unless he repents, will have to pay for his sins. The man who kills will also have to pay, for even though he can make many justifications for doing so, it is still a sin. God is the only judge, and it does not matter whether sins are approved by man. It is to God you will have to answer."

The man lowered his stick and said to his friend, "Come on, let's go. He's learned his lesson. Leave him to these beggars." They turned and left, feeling unsure of themselves.

Peter was kneeling beside the man holding his head in his arms, while Matthew wiped the man's face with a cloth. Peter looked to John and said, "Bring some water to clean his wounds."

Matthew said, "I don't think he will live much longer, Master. They have beaten him so much he cannot survive." I came to the man and knelt down beside him, stroking his brow. His eyes flickered open and he said in a weak voice, "Have they gone?"

"Yes, My friend, they are gone," I replied, softly.

"Sir, I heard what You said, and before I die, I would like to ask God's forgiveness for what I have done," he whispered.

"God loves you, My child, and only offers you goodness and rest," I said.

He moved a little and groaned with pain as he did. The tears welled in My eyes to see him suffer so, and to see what man could do to man.

"I have no one else to tell, so I will tell You my sins, as I feel I must admit before God my wrongs. I have been a thief, a liar, a cheat. I have taken advantage of so many without a thought, but now I see it was wrong. I see how I have hurt so many. I pray to God for His, and their, forgiveness, and I accept my fate as payment for my sins," he said, and then his eyes began to close again.

"My friend, you have spoken truly, and from your heart. Today the forgiveness of God is with you," I said, lovingly, to him. As I leaned forward to kiss his forehead, he took his last breath, saying, "Mother," and died.

My disciples looked at Me and said, "Master, could You not have healed him?"

"His time had come, and soon he is to be welcomed in Heaven by My Father," I said, as tears rolled down My cheeks.

"How could he go to Heaven?" said Judas Iscariot. "He is a sinner."

"All mankind sins, but this man knew his sins and truly repented of them. How could My Father deny him? I tell you, he will sit in Heaven as a gift of love from Me to My Father."

Peter was sobbing and John looked broken hearted as the sun rose and showed us how severely he had been beaten. I looked to Heaven with a heavy heart and said, "Father, forgive this child of Yours, and welcome him into Your heart." We all began to pray for him, and then we laid him to rest at the side of the road.

Later as we walked, Judas said to Peter, "I still don't understand how a sinner could go to Heaven."

Peter, still visibly upset turned to him and said, "If that is so, how do you expect to go there?"

Judas quickly left Peter and walked on in deep thought.

J
E
J E S U S
U
S

Jesus ††† 4-7-96

The morning air was fresh, and there was a dew on the ground as the sun rose and shone brightly.

"Lord," said Simon (not Peter), "it is wonderful how the dew glistens on the plants as the sun shines on it...look see?" I looked and saw the beauty that Simon spoke of.

"Simon, if you can see each of the dew drops as the soul of man, you would see in the dark they are hidden, but when the light of the Son touches them, they shine brightly and become as little jewels." Simon looked deeply at the dew drops and then turned to Me, saying, "Yes, they are so beautiful. They do look like jewels. Wouldn't it be nice if mankind were so beautiful."

"They can be, if only they would submit themselves in complete obedience to God. Then, filled with God's love, they, too, would shine so brightly," I replied.

"It seems so hard for many to do that," interrupted Matthew, who was now also by My side.

"It is not as hard as many believe. If only they would try, they would see it can be as simple as the dew drop letting the sun light it up. All they have to do is to let the Son's love shine through them and in them. Then they will find the strength that makes the burden light," I responded. We walked on talking more about God's love and how it will illuminate souls if it is accepted without conditions.

Ahead of us was a group of merchants heading home from the markets in Capernaum. They turned and looked at us, wondering if we were thieves coming to rob them.

"Peace," I said raising My hand in greeting, and as My love touched them in My word, they became full of trust.

"Welcome," called their leader in return. "Where are you going?" he asked.

"To the next village," said Peter.

"To pray in the synagogue and heal the sick," said Judas, proudly, and seeming slightly taller than normal.

"You can heal the sick?" asked the man, as his companions looked at each other.

"Yes," replied Judas, looking so important. "The Master heals the blind, the deaf, the lame. He can heal anyone!" shouted Judas excitedly.

"Judas," I said calmly, "let us be humble in the presence of others. Let us be humble in our lives. Pride only brings sin, whereas humility brings peace."

"I only wanted them to know who You are, Lord, so that they, too, could share in Your love," said Judas, somewhat deflated now.

"If you are to bring others to Me, it is to be done in humility. Anyone who comes to Me and follows Me, must be humble. Otherwise, they are not being My true friends and My true followers. Humility is the Way, for in humility, God's will is fulfilled."

"Well said!" cried the merchants' leader, as he came forward and knelt before Me. "My name is Joseph, and I have a son who is sick. He is here with us. Can You please help, Lord?"

"What is wrong with him?" asked Peter.

"He drank some bad wine and he looks as if he will die. The physicians could not cure him, and now, with sadness in my heart, I take him home to his mother to die," said the man crying before Me.

"Bring him to Me," I said leaning down touching the man softly. Two men came forward helping a young man, no more than eighteen. He could not stand by himself and was vomiting blood. Judas stepped back in disgust.

As they brought him to Me, I embraced him and said, "Be filled with the love of God and live your life for God."

As I said this he stopped vomiting, stood up straight, and looked as if nothing had been wrong with him. His father rushed to him, embracing him and crying, "My son, my son." The son looked into My eyes, fell to his knees and said, "Master, can I follow You in thanks to God for His mercy?"

"One day you will be needed to help. Until then be with your family." He looked at Me, disappointed at first, then smiling, said, "What is it I will be needed for, my Lord?"

"One day a Man will be hanging on a cross. He will have given His life for others. Below the cross will be His Mother, broken hearted, and waiting to hold her Son's body. You will help then, by taking His body from the cross and laying Him in His Mother's arms," I replied.

His father said, "Lord, I will be there to help also, if I am needed."

"You will be, Joseph, and your name will be remembered throughout time," I said, smiling at him.

"Have You eaten yet?" asked the son.

"No," said Judas quickly, "and I am starving."

"Join us for a meal then," said Joseph, and we shared a pleasant breakfast, after which we parted to go our separate ways.

J
E
J E S U S
U
S

Jesus ††† 4-8-96

"They were nice people," commented Andrew as he and James walked with Me.

"Yes, I enjoyed sharing a meal with them," I answered.

"Master, did You see how much Judas ate. He must be preparing for a long time without food," said

45.

James with a look of amazement on his face. I looked at Judas, who was walking before Me holding his stomach and looking full.

"Greed can be a destroyer of men, whether it is greed for goods or for money. Whatever it is you are greedy for, in your greed you deny others and you grow in thoughts of self," I said, feeling a little sad for Judas, who suddenly turned to face Me and said, "Master, I did enjoy that food...so much of it...it was a feast. I could have eaten just a little more if there was time. It was a shame we had to finish so quickly."

He could see no wrong in his behavior, and thought no more of it. I said nothing, as I had been a little hard on Judas at times, and did love him so.

James spoke up, "Master, do you ever wonder how people can be so blind?"

"James, the blindness you see comes from a blindness within. I came to bring sight to the blind, the blind of spirit as well as the blind of sight. Sometimes, however, the sight cannot be restored, because some refuse to accept the healing offered. Imagine if you were hungry and a man with plenty of food offered you some, but you refused...you would remain hungry. What you needed was there, but you rejected it so you remain as you are, hungry.

"This is how so many are today. They are offered God's healing love. It is there for them but they choose not to reach out and take it, so they remain blind to the truth," I answered.

James and Andrew were both looking at Me, then Andrew said, "Lord, Your knowledge is so great, I wonder if I will ever learn enough?"

"You will learn by the Spirit of knowledge and truth that will come upon you in the future," I said, gently putting My arms around them both, and together we began to praise God.

J
e
J e s u s
u
s

Jesus ††† 4-14-96

Our prayers encouraged the others to join in, and now we were all praising the Father as we walked the road. As we turned the bend we saw the town before us. It seemed so quiet. We entered the town and no one was in sight, and as we walked on, we saw why. There was a funeral procession and all the townspeople seemed to be there. Four men were carrying a dead young man for burial.

The sobbing of the women broke My heart... so much sadness, so much despair. "He was so young," a woman cried. "Why did he have to die?" she sobbed. We came closer to the dead man. His face was so peaceful, so calm.

"Why cry for the sleeping?" I said.

"He is dead!" shouted many in anger. "Can't You see he is dead, are You mad?" someone hissed.

"Do you believe in God?" I asked, calmly.

"Of course we do," was the reply.

"Do you believe in Abraham, your father?" I asked again.

"Yes, yes, we do," they said.

"Then, do you believe that Abraham waits for you in death, and that Yahweh will give you only goodness and joy if you have lived a good life?" I quizzed.

"Yes, yes, we do. What's Your point?" said someone.

"Well, if you believe that, and this man has lived a good life, why are you sad?" There was silence for a moment, even the sobbing had stopped.

"Death is not the end, it is but a step to your new life with God. I know so often in death, only the sadness of a lost family member or friend is seen. You long for them to be with you, you miss them, your life does not seem to be complete any more. There is a hole in your life, and you feel so lonely at times. See, though, that these are your feelings, your needs...and see that it is natural to feel this way, for in your love of the dead, you want them with you always. Try to understand, though, that the new life in God that good people come to in death, is the greatest reward, the greatest joy you can ever have. If you can understand this just a little, you will find death not so painful, and you will understand what a gift it is...a special gift from God for the good, and an eternal ordeal for the bad," I said.

They all looked dumbfounded, and so I said, "God, who is love, is the giver of life and is the taker of life. It is by God's will that all exist, and to glorify My Father in Heaven, who is life itself, I will offer My life to show the truth in death.

"Now I say to this man: 'Arise and be free of death until you are called by My Father. Arise and glorify God with your every breath.'"

I leaned over and kissed him on the cheek as his eyes flickered open and he sat up.

"Where am I?" he said, looking around him at the crowd, who was still silent. "I am hungry, can I have some food?" he said. The crowd broke into joyous laughter and embraced him.

They started to praise God at the top of their voices, and we slipped out of the village unnoticed in the commotion. As we left we could hear, "Where is He? Where has He gone?"

"Master, why didn't we stay?" said James, at My side. "It is better for them to be left to enjoy this gift together. In time, they will understand what God gave them in this miracle and in My words," I said. We walked on in silence with My disciples thinking of what had just happened.

J
E
J E S U S
U
S

Jesus ††† 4-19-96

Dusk was approaching as we sat together around a fire we made by the side of the road. Andrew stood up and stretching his arms out, gave a big yawn. "I am so tired Master. Shouldn't we find somewhere quiet to stay for awhile, so we can rest and recover from the past days?"

"Andrew, sit down and don't worry the Master," said Peter, who was always ready to protect me from minor problems.

"Peter, Andrew is right. We are tired as we have been working hard since we left the inn," said Judas who always wanted to rest.

"It is up to the Master when we should rest," cried John, My dear friend.

"I can go on forever, if Jesus asks me," shouted James, in youthful fervor.

As I was about to answer, snoring started from Bartholomew who had fallen asleep through the noise. "It seems Bartholomew has made the decision for us. We will sleep here tonight, and in the morning we will go to Judah to rest," I said. I smiled at how Bartholomew could have fallen asleep with the others' loud voices making so much noise.

Judas opened the purse, then looking at Me, said, "Master we do not have much money left. How can we stay in Judah with so little?"

Peter stood up angrily, "There was plenty there yesterday. Where has it all gone?"

"I don't know," wailed Judas. "This is all there is now. Look!"

"I don't need to look. I know what happened. The same as always happens. It just disappears into thin air," snapped Peter.

Judas shrank back, "I-I-I don't know what you mean," he said.

"Oh yes you do," said John, looking disappointingly at Judas. Judas looked at Me pleadingly.

"It does not matter," I said, "it is only money, My Father will provide all we need."

"But Master, the money is always disappearing," said Peter, still angry.

"Peter, if you get so angry over money, how can you say you are any different from those in the synagogues today? So often we see how money takes them away from God. Will it happen to you also, My friends?"

Peter, now looking at the ground, replied, "I am sorry Master. It is so easy to worry about unimportant things. It is so easy to forget what you teach us. Will I ever learn? I am so stupid."

I put my arm around him and said, "You are not stupid. You are human and sometimes you go wrong, but learn from these times. Your faith is strong but sometimes you let your passion take hold. If you can control that, you will find you become a rock that stands firm against the evil in the world."

Peter looked up at Me and smiled, saying, "You are so forgiving Lord. I wish I could be like that."

"You will be. You will be," I assured him.

During the night I woke to see Judas leaving us quietly. I knew where he was going. It was where he always went. He went to hide some of the donations he hid on himself during the day. I felt sad to see how money could destroy a soul...how it starts in a little way, and then gets larger and larger. All of a sudden money seems to mean everything. Money is given great importance and everything else is secondary.

This is how Satan works. Money and wealth are gifts that can be used for good when they are shared, or for evil when they are used for self and power. How clever the evil one is, turning what can be used for good into an instrument of evil that takes My children deeper into his clutches.

Isn't this always the way of evil, taking gifts that are for all mankind, and causing a few to believe they are only for them? Then what they have isn't enough and they want more. What they do not see is that when they have more, someone else has less.

They do not see how they hurt others and themselves. They do not see how sometimes they cause others to sin, for if others have little, in their weakness, they may sin to get more in order to be like the wealthy.

No sin is seen in what they do, for it is their right to take what is theirs, regardless of the consequences. What foolish men, and what a foolish Judas, as he follows the path of evil. How sad! I closed My eyes and slept a troubled sleep thinking of My friend Judas, whom I loved so much.

J
E
J E S U S
U
S

Jesus ††† 4-29-96

I awoke with thoughts of My Mother, whom I had not seen for some time. I thought of her at home waiting for Me to return. As My disciples awoke, I said to them, "It is time to return to Nazareth, as I would like to visit My Mother."

"Wonderful," said Peter happily, "Your Mother Mary always welcomes us, as if we were her own children."

"Yes, Lord, and how she cooks," said Judas who had a deep love for My Mother because she always treated him with love...the love of a mother. Judas carried on saying, "I love to visit Your home, Master. The few times I have been there, I didn't want to leave."

"That is how it is for all those who come to My house to visit My Mother. She welcomes them and makes them feel at home, as if this is where they truly belong. My Mother opens her heart to all of My family and makes them her own, and one day mankind will come to understand how important My Mother is in the salvation of souls," I said, as we all started to collect our belongings for the journey ahead.

"Master," said James, "how long will it take to reach Nazareth?"

"It is not far, James, maybe two days walking," I replied.

"Master, will You do me the honor, then, of allowing me to carry Your belongings, so that You will not be so tired when You see Your Mother?" asked James.

I looked into his heart and saw the deep love and the concern he had, that I should be able to enjoy every moment at My home. "James, My dear friend, I will gladly let you carry My burden, for it is by accepting some of what I have to carry, that you share in My work."

James looked puzzled at what I had said, but he joyfully picked up My belongings, and almost danced as he walked with them in his arms.

He started to sing a happy song that he had learned in his childhood, about the love that My Father has for His children and, as the others joined in, the mood became festive. The singing got louder and louder as they opened their hearts in expressing their love of their Father in Heaven.

J
E
J E S U S
U
S

Jesus ††† 5-31-96

As we walked along singing and praying, time passed so quickly. Before we knew, it was dusk and time to settle for the evening. What a wonderful day it had been. My disciples totally absorbed in prayer and worship. I felt very happy.

As we sat by the fire we had made, I could see My friends were tired. They thought the tiredness came from the walking. They did not understand that the day's prayers had also taken their toll, for as they pray, they enter the battle between good and evil...a constant battle. The tiredness that comes from this fight is a spiritual tiredness, a tiredness that many do not recognize. Often, it is seen as one's body being exhausted from the day's toil. The spirit is not seen as being tired, and so sometimes it goes unnoticed.

Just as a tired body needs rest, so does the spirit. Just as a hungry body needs food, so does the soul. But oh, so many, even devout people, do not understand this. I turned to My followers and said, "Gather together and join hands, for I will pray to the Father that the Holy Spirit will give you the strength you need to be My disciples." They did as I asked and waited in silent expectation.

"Father, I ask You now through the Holy Spirit to strengthen those You have given Me, so that they may walk tirelessly along the way." As I said these words the spirit's of My disciples' were touched and refreshed by the love of the Holy Spirit. After this renewal, they all slept soundly until morning. Looking upon them asleep, I saw many of those who would follow...those who would exhaust themselves spiritually as well as physically, and not recognize it.

I knew also that the food and the strength they needed would be there for them, as I would supply it in a perpetual sacrifice, given to nourish spirits and save souls. All it would take is for them to accept this sacrifice, and to eat of it in faith...a faith that sees Me in every sacramental offering, a faith that opens the heart to God.

J
E
J E S U S
U
S

Jesus †††   6-1-96

Morning broke and as the sun shone down upon us, My disciples began to collect their belongings preparing for the walk ahead.

James and John came to Me, and John spoke, "Master, it will not be long now until You see Your Mother. James and I wondered if the rest of us should camp a little away from Your home for the first night, so that You may have time alone with her?"

I looked at both of them and saw the true love they had for Me, a love that would be tested many times in the future. "My friends," I said, "it is very thoughtful of you and I thank you for your concern, but you need not be uncomfortable. I will find time to be alone with My Mother."

They smiled softly at Me and turned to finish collecting their belongings. I heard James whisper to John, "He is so kind. He never lets us suffer unless He shares it with us." Little did he know the truth in what he said.

As we walked, Peter and Matthew were by My side. Peter discussed how simple it was for men to be deceived, and how easily men could turn their backs on God.

Matthew, ever the thinker, listened intently and then said, "Yes, it is so, Peter, but what you must remember is that we have the Lord to show us the way; most people don't. Remember how you were before the Master came to you; that is how people are who have not heard or known the Lord. I hope one day the whole world knows what we do, so that they can understand what God's love really means."

Peter looked hurt thinking about how he was before. Matthew saw this and said, "Master, we were all so far away from God until You showed us the truth. I can hardly believe what I was like before, and yet, even now I am not much better."

Peter smiled. He knew Matthew said this for his benefit.

"My friends, it does no good to look back at the way you were. What matters is how you are now and what you will be in times to come. As for the people who are confused and turn from God, one day they will be offered forgiveness and a guiding hand to bring them back to God. Just as you, they will need only to accept the truth to find salvation," I said, thinking about the generations to come.

Peter looked at Me, and said, "Lord, I hope many will be saved."

"So do I," said Matthew, "and I hope many will come to know You, Lord."

We walked on in silence. Then Judas came to Me and said, "Master, can we rest soon? Is it much further now? I am so tired."

"Judas!" snapped Peter, "We have only been walking a few hours. Do not bother the Master."

"Judas," I said, smiling softly, "I know your burden is heavy, and at times it makes you weary. Here, let Me carry some for you."

Judas looked shocked and said, "No, Master, it is all right, I can carry it but I just thought we should rest."

"One day your burden will be so much that you will be unable to carry it by yourself. On that day I will be waiting to help, if you only ask Me. Don't be embarrassed, as you are today. I am your friend and no matter what happens I will be there for you, if you just ask," I replied, gently.

Judas looked totally confused. He wondered when he would have so much to carry and why. Poor Judas; if only he understood.

J
E
J E S U S
U
S

Jesus ††† 6-2-96

We walked into the afternoon, and then in the distance up a hill was Nazareth and My home. My heart filled with joy at the thought of being with My Mother again, and the thought of her love for Me. "My friends, soon we will be at My Mother's house. Let us praise the Father as we take these last steps home," I said, happily, and together we started to praise the Father.

As we came to the outskirts of Nazareth, there were children playing and dogs barking in the excitement of the game. Some of the children stopped playing and looked at us as we walked towards them. Then one cried, "It is Jesus," and they ran to greet Me.

They walked with us to My Mother's house jumping with joy and excitement. One child asked, "Jesus, will You tell us of Your travels?" I put My hand on his head and stroked his hair saying, "Of course I will, but tomorrow, for first I must see My Mother."

They all started to shout, "Tell us a story, tell us a story." I stopped and sat on a nearby wall, telling the children to sit on the ground before Me. "I will tell you a short story now, but tomorrow I will spend more time with you," I said.

Simon came forward and said into My ear, "Master, there are more important things to do than to tell children stories. Why spend so much time with them?"

I looked at him and replied, "Simon, do you not see the pure love and innocence children have? This is how all should be. If I spend time with them it is because of the joy they bring Me. Also, the love that I will place in their pure open hearts will help them become, in later life, the good people they were created to be. The children of today are the adults of tomorrow, adults who should remain as children, pure and innocent."

Simon said, "Sorry, Lord, forgive me," and then he sat among the children, embracing two of them.

I started to tell them a story of love. "One day there was a young boy who loved his mother and father dearly. He was a good boy, praying often, always respecting his elders, and friendly to everyone. As he played with his friends one morning they came across a bag of coins. Filled with excitement, they started to think of how the money could help their poor families, how they might be able to buy toys and new clothes. They had so many thoughts of what they could do with the money.

Then the good boy spoke up saying. "This money is not ours. We should try to find out to whom it belongs. Otherwise we are stealing."

The other children started to shout at him, "You are crazy. This is no one's. It is ours. We found it."

He insisted, "No, it is not ours. Someone has lost it, and we should return it." The other children started to beat him and laughed at him, but he would not change his mind.

He kept saying, "It is stealing. It is wrong."

The other children kept beating and beating him until he was unconscious. Then they stopped and looked at each other saying, "What have we done? We have killed him. Quick, get help!"

Some ran to the boy's house and called his parents. Others took him in their arms and wiped his face. The oldest boy in the group started to cry, and looking to Heaven said, "Oh God, we are sorry for what we did. Please don't let him die. We don't want this money. I will give up all of my toys and clothes, if only You will let him live."

The other children joined in asking for God's help, and the one holding the bag of money threw it away saying, "We don't want this, Lord. We want our friend back."

The unconscious boy's eyes flickered open, and he stood up a little dazed. All the children came around him, hugging and kissing him. They said they were sorry and asked forgiveness. The good boy said, "My friends, of course I forgive you, because I love you and you are my friends."

Just then his parents arrived, and seeing their son badly beaten, rushed to him and embraced him. They asked what had happened. After being told of the events, they looked at the children before them. The children looked so scared and were crying. At first his parents felt angry. Then they were sad for all the children, not only their son.

The father spoke, "Show me this money." So the child who had thrown it away went to look for it, but could not find it. It was gone.

The father said to the children, "I hope you have learned a lesson today. Do you see how easily the thoughts of wealth can destroy the love in your heart, how evil the greed for money can be, how it can lead you to sin, to hurt each other. The true wealth in life is the love of God and the love you have for each other. Without that, life is empty."

The children sobbed, "We know. We threw the money away. We don't want it. We are sorry for what we did."

The mother of the boy said, "Children, it is so easy to be confused and to be led away from a good life. I think today you have learned this. My son suffered at your hands because of thoughts of greed, but his suffering is over now. Your's however will be on your hearts for a long time."

She looked at her son who was smiling at her. He said to her, "Mother, can they come home with me for they are my friends?" The mother smiled at all the children and said, "Wipe your tears. Let's go to my house where, with my son, we can celebrate your friendship."

The father picked up his son and placed him on his shoulder, asking, "Are you all right, son?"

"Yes, father," he replied, "I have those around me who love me, and whom I love. What more could I ask for?"

As I looked before Me I could see the children intrigued, when one of them jumped up and said, "What about the money? What happened to it?"

"Does it matter?" I said, "What was important was the love among them. All the money did was to damage this love."

The child sat down as Judas spoke up, "I would have liked to have found that bag."

Everyone turned and looked at him as he went red in the face.

"The money only brought suffering. If this is what it does, it is better to be poor and happy," said Thomas.

"Yes, but money can make you happy if it fills your stomach, and gives you a nice bed to lie in," retorted Judas, thinking of our travels.

"Money," I said, "can be a destroyer or a builder. If it is used for good, it is welcome, but if it is used for self, it should be rejected. Money is not what makes life happy, it is the heart of the person. Money...so hard at times to live without it, but much harder to live with it. When money hardens your heart, then it hurts you and others."

As I entered the doorway of My house, I looked to see Mother busy cooking. She turned suddenly, surprised to see Me. She said, "Jesus!" and smiled. I went over to her and put My arms around her. "Mother, it is good to see you again. I have missed you," I said, happy to be home.

My Mother put her head against My chest saying, "I have missed You, too, my Son, I am glad You have come to visit me. You must be hungry. Sit down and I will bring You something," she said. As she kissed My cheek, she said, "I will prepare a meal for Your followers as well."

"Mother, it is so good to be home. I always feel your love filling My heart when I am here. Often at night when I am away, I think of how you held Me as a child, and how you loved Me from your heart," I said, thinking of the past.

"I also cherish those moments, my Son, when we were together with Joseph as a family living in God's love," replied Mother.

I pondered, "Ah, Joseph, My dear protector, My guardian, My guide in My youth. Joseph, so humble, so loving, such a man among men, a gift to the world, a gift of quiet service and love."

"Call Your friends in," said Mother. A tear ran from her eye, as she thought of Joseph. Raising her hand to wipe it away, she said, "I so loved Joseph, and I do miss him, but I know he is happy and we will all be together again with the Father in Heaven."

I went outside and said to My friends, "My Mother is preparing a meal for us. Let us go to the synagogue for a little while and offer our prayers in thanks for her love."

Mother came to Me and said, "But, Jesus, You are hungry. Eat just a little now to keep You until You return."

I turned and embraced her, saying joyfully, "Mother, you always worry about Me. I won't be long, and then I will eat and make you happy." I kissed her on the cheek and headed for the synagogue, which was not far away. Mother shouted after Me, "Don't be too long, my Son. We have so much to talk about."

I looked back and smiled, as I saw each of My disciples giving My Mother a kiss before following Me to the synagogue. My Mother, a true mother to all.

After praying, we returned to My house where Mother set out a wonderful meal for us. "Come in, come in," she said to My friends, as they stood in the doorway. "Find yourself a place, and make yourselves comfortable. You know I love having all of you here. To me you are all my children."

Peter replied, "And we all think of you as our mother." The others joined in agreement. Smiling at Mother I said, "You certainly have a big family, but I know your heart is big enough for many, many more."

The meal was delicious, just as I remembered the meals at home. Over the table, My disciples told My Mother of the many things that had happened since we last saw her.

She listened to each one so intently as if she loved each word they spoke, and all of them were so at ease in My Mother's love. I smiled as I thought of how she would love all people in the future, how she would listen to each person, as a mother listens to her child, and how she would always be there for everyone. I saw also how her pure love touched those around her and filled them with joy. What a special gift My Father has given the world in My Mother, a gift that is for all, a gift that all should recognize, and a gift for which everyone should thank God.

Time passed quickly in the enjoyment of the evening, and soon many fell asleep. My Mother Mary, went to each one and covered them to make sure they would not be cold during the night. Then she came and sat next to Me, looking at those asleep.

"Jesus, my Son," she said, "when I look upon these men, I see little boys who need to be loved. It is the same when I look upon others in the markets. In the streets, they all seem like little children. Some seem so confused, some lost, but they all seem to be looking for love, and I just want to give them that love, so that they can find their way in life and their way to God.

"My Son, I thank Our Father in Heaven for giving me such a wonderful gift...a gift that makes me love everyone as my own."

I put My head onto her lap and she began to stroke My hair. "I think it should be mankind who thanks God for what they have been given in you, Mother," I said as I drifted into sleep.

J
e
J e s u s
u
s

Jesus ††† 6-3-96

When I awoke early in the morning, I saw My Mother kneeling in the corner and praying to the Father. Each word she said filled My heart with joy. Each prayer touched My heart in a special way, and, joined with the Father and the Holy Spirit, I sat silently letting Mother's prayers fill Me.

After awhile, she stopped praying, and started to read some sheets with Psalms on them. I walked over to her and sat beside her, joining in the words. Smiling, Mother looked at me with love radiating from her. I whispered, "I love these times when you come in prayer to God. Your voice and your words are sweetness itself."

Mother looked embarrassed for a moment, but then put her arms around Me, and we continued to read the Psalms. The sound of our voices woke My followers, and one by one, they joined in prayer with us. Soon the house was filled with praise and thanks to God. I saw how My Mother, by her prayers, had led others into prayer and praise of God, and I knew this is how it would be for many in the future...My Mother leading them deeper and deeper into a prayerful life.

After we finished our prayers, Mother Mary said, "I will prepare some food as you all must be hungry." James jumped to his feet. "Mother," he said boyishly, "let us prepare something for you. You have done so much already."

She came to him and putting her arm around his shoulders said, "My son, you are always so willing to help. What a good boy you are."

James looked very happy, and said, "What can I do?"

"If you could go to the well for some water, that would help," replied Mother. James grabbed the water jug, and swinging it as he walked out the door, said, "I won't be long."

Andrew, who was helping Mother with the meal, saw there was only a little food, barely enough to feed us all.

Andrew said to her, "Excuse me, Mother Mary, I must go out for awhile." She looked at him, saying, "Well, don't be long, or you may not get anything to eat."

Andrew went over to Judas and whispered quietly to him. Judas smiled, and handed something to him. Judas loved My Mother so he never would deny her, even though he would, and did, deny so many others.

As Andrew left, James returned with the water.

"Where is Andrew going?" he asked.

"Don't worry about that," said Bartholomew, "he will be back soon."

Mother finished preparing the meal and Andrew had not yet returned. She divided a small amount of the food among us, and put some to one side for

Andrew. Judas spoke up, "You have left none for yourself, Mother."

She looked at him and said, "It is all right, I will eat later. You need food to give you strength for the work you do." All the disciples looked at the small meal before them and understood this was all My Mother had, and that she would go hungry for them.

Peter looked up and said, "You give us such a feast. Here, share it with us."

He started to put some of his food on a plate for her, and the others did the same, while Judas kept looking at the door. All of a sudden, a large smile came across Judas' face, as he saw Andrew at the door with a big bag in his hands. We all looked at Andrew as he said, "Mother, we thought, as we have eaten so much of your food and you have made us so welcome, we should at least replace what we have eaten."

He opened the bag and brought out enough food to last for a month. "Oh, my children," said Mother, as a tear rolled down her cheek, "you spoil me."

James jumped up and began to sing with a joyful voice, "A gift of love for our Mother. A gift of love for our Mother." He danced around the room so happy. Then he went to Mother and said, "Sit down now, and let me prepare you a meal."

She sat down looking so pleased, grateful for the love My followers showed her. I smiled at them. They were like little children bringing a gift to their Mother.

I hoped all mankind would be like this and could see that My Mother would do anything to help them. She would even give her own without complaining...a true Mother's love. I wanted all mankind to see how important My Mother was in their lives, and I wanted everyone to treat her with love and respect as My disciples did. Yes, even Judas.

There was a call from outside. "Is it true Jesus is home?" I recognized the booming voice of Emial, a friend I had grown up with. I walked outside to see him. He had a large smile on his face.

"Jesus, why didn't You tell me You were here?" he said, as he rushed forward and embraced Me in his big arms. "I only arrived last evening," I started to say, but before I could finish he carried on, "How long will You stay, my friend? I have seen so little of You these past years."

"Only a few days, then we must be on our way," I replied.

"Still taking that wonderful love, and those great words of Yours, to the people, eh?" he said, half as a question and half as a statement. I could not help but love him, so open, so friendly, so loving... a gentle giant of a man with a booming voice and a big heart.

I remembered when we went to another village once, and the boys there made fun of Me for going to the synagogue to pray. How Emial stood between us, and they threw stones at him and cut his face before they ran away. He would not listen to My thanks, as he said, "That is what friends are for." Emial...a good friend.

"Come and visit my house. I am married now, and soon we will have a child," he asked, with a hopeful look in his eyes. "My wife longs to meet You. I have told her so much about You. She is a good woman."

"Of course, I will, My friend. How could I not come to your home, for I love you?" I answered.

He looked even happier now. "Wonderful! Wonderful! Bring Your friends and I can tell them of Your youth," he boomed.

"We will go to the synagogue first, and then we will visit you, Emial, My friend," I responded.

"I will go and tell my wife. She will be so happy to see You," he said, as he turned and walked away.

"Jesus," Mary said, "he is a good man. Every day he comes to see me, just to say hello, so he says...but I know he is watching over me. He has married a beautiful woman but she cannot walk, so he does all of the chores, as well as the farm work to earn their keep.

"When the baby comes he does not know what he will do. But even through all this, he is happy and in love with his wife...a truly good man." Mother looked into My heart and I could see her request within Me.

I said, "Yes, he was always happy no matter what happened, and he always wanted to help people...a kind man and a gentle soul."

In the synagogue, I sat quietly listening to the words of My Father, and feeling the warmth of the Holy Spirit. After some hours, I said to Peter, "Come, let us go to My friend's house."

We left the synagogue, and stopped at the market to buy some food and gifts for My friend's family. Emial stood outside his house waiting for us.

"Jesus," he said in his truthful way, "You took so long, I wondered if You would come."

"Emial, how could I forget you?" I said. He smiled and, looking to the ground, said, "Since I got married not many visit us now. I think they are embarrassed."

"Then they are not true friends, for between friends, there are no barriers," I said, putting My arm around his broad shoulders.

"Come in," he said, happily, to my followers. "I hope you will all fit into my small house." We did fit inside with plenty of room to spare. Sitting on the floor by the table was his wife. She had such a beautiful face, and her eyes shone brightly, but her body was twisted horribly. Her arms stuck out at awkward angles. Her feet were tangled beneath her, and she looked to be in pain.

"This is my wife, Miriam. Isn't she beautiful?" he said, smiling at her. "And this is my friend, Jesus, whom I told you so much about."

"Jesus," she said, and smiled at Me. I could see how ashamed of herself she felt...how she thought it would hurt her husband, as his friends turned their backs on him again.

"Miriam, such a beautiful name and such a lovely smile," I said, feeling a deep love for her. My apostles warmly greeted her, and some embraced her. Judas stayed back and said nothing. He looked with disgust at the crippled woman before him.

Emial rushed around saying, "Sit, sit." On the table was the finest fruit. It must have been a big expense for him. He brought jugs of wine and water, which we all enjoyed, except Judas, who thought it was cheap wine.

Emial was full of joy recounting some of the many childhood adventures we had. It fascinated My disciples that he could be happy over the smallest thing. He picked up Miriam and placed her on his knees. Then he said, "The happiest moment in my life was when I married my wife. She is so beautiful, and now she carries our child." Judas shuddered, but everyone else was happy.

I looked at Miriam and saw that the boy child within her was dead. I looked at my friend and saw so much hope in his heart. Then I looked at Miriam, so frightened of people, so unsure if these men really like her. I saw the hurt in her eyes from Judas' reactions, which most had not noticed, but she had.

My heart cried for these friends of Mine, when I said, "Emial, may I hold Miriam for a moment?" He looked at me, wondering at first if I would hurt her, but knowing Me, he gave her gently to Me. I held her in My arms and kissed her cheeks. She started to cry, as I said, "My Father, My friend is here before You with his family of love. I, Your Son, ask of You to fill this family with Your mercy, and let the love in their hearts become Your healing love." I closed My eyes for a moment calling from My heart to My Father. Then I said, "Miriam, all that is in you and all that is you, be healed, in the mercy of God."

I placed her on the floor, and with tears of joy she came to her feet, and her arms were straightened. The child within her came to life. Emial rushed to her shouting, "Miriam, Miriam, Miriam!" He picked her up in his arms and carried on shouting, "Praise God, thank You Father, thank You Jesus, praise God!"

My disciples joined in praising God, as both Emial and Miriam fell before Me and kissed My feet. I bent down and helped them up. "There is no need for that, My friends. Just praise God with the rest of your lives and your children's lives."

"Jesus, how can I ever thank You?" said My friend.

"By living as you are, pure and happy, and by offering every day to God. Also, tell no one of this, for it is not yet time for them to know." Miriam, kissing My hand, said "We will, Lord, we will. I promise, I promise." Judas, in the corner, looked on in disbelief.

Later that evening, we went back to the synagogue to thank My Father, after which we returned home to My Mother. As I entered the door she said "Thank you, Jesus," and kissed Me. My disciples started to tell her what happened but there was no surprise in her eyes, only thanks and love.

J
e
J e s u s
u
s

Jesus ††† 6-8-96

We sat talking with My Mother until early in the morning. What joy she brought with her smiles, her concern, her love, and giving of herself to keep us comfortable. My Mother told My disciples stories of My youth, stories of how Joseph trusted in God through difficult moments, and stories of how, even through hardships, her life was a complete joy. What an example to all mankind on how to live, how to love, and how to give.

The morning broke and again I was with Mother praying and worshipping the Father. After prayer, I was a little sad as I knew soon we would leave My home. There was so much to do, so many to save, and so many to heal. Over the morning meal, My Mother said, with a softness in her voice that hid the sadness, "Soon it will be time for You to leave me, so eat well to prepare You for Your journey."

My disciples were unusually quiet until James spoke, "Mother Mary, I will be sad to leave. I always enjoy being here with you, but I also will be happy to leave, for I know we go to do God's work. Isn't it strange how I can be happy yet sad?"

Such wisdom in a young man I thought, before I said, "Often it is that way when you give for God.

Often sorrow and joy are almost one, the sorrow of so many sinners and their sins, with the joy of saving them. The suffering needed to defeat evil and the glory in the victory over evil. This is the way of God... sometimes a hard way, but always the best and most rewarding way."

Later as we were preparing to leave, a young boy came to My Mother's house and spoke to Mother saying, "Jesus promised He would tell us a story before He left. Please ask Him to come and tell us one now." My Mother stroked the boy's hair, and said, "He will come soon. Don't worry, Jesus never forgets a promise." Then she looked at Me and smiled.

"I will meet you all as I leave the village. I have not forgotten, I will be there soon," I said. Mother came to Me and kissed Me saying, "There are so many demands on Your time, make sure You look after Yourself and take time to rest."

"I will, Mother," I said. As I embraced her I could feel her tears falling on My neck. My disciples all made their farewells as we departed, with My Mother watching us leave. The children were waiting, and as we came toward them they were calling, "Jesus, Jesus, Jesus." I sat among them, as did My disciples.

"There was a man," I began, "who was a leper, and all the people kept away from him, fearing they might catch his disease. One day as the leper walked the road, he came across some people who had had an accident. There were two men and a woman, and the cart they were traveling in had turned over. One man was trapped underneath it. Both the other two had broken bones.

"The leper came closer to them and shouted, 'I am a leper, but if there is anything I can do to help, I will.'"

"'Go away!' shouted the woman, 'You are diseased. Go away!' The man with the broken bones had some stones in his hand, and he started to throw them at the leper, who still offered his help. The man trapped beneath the cart said to the others, 'Leave him alone, he only offers his help. Even though he suffers, he thinks of us.'"

"'I don't want his sickness,' said the woman.

"'Neither do I' said the other man.

67.

"'I think he is healthier than any of us,' said the trapped man, 'for he has a good charitable heart, which I do not see in us.' Then he called to the leper, 'You can help me if you would. I cannot move. This cart has me trapped.' The leper came to the cart as the others crawled away saying, 'Don't touch us.'

"'You are stuck well there, my friend,' said the leper, 'but I think I can help.' He went and collected the two horses and, tying a rope on them and then to the cart, he lifted it from the man. As he rose to his feet with hardly any injuries, the trapped man smiled at the leper saying, 'Thank you, my friend.' With that he came forward and placed a large bag of coins in the leper's hand, as he said, 'I can do nothing for your illness but maybe this will bring you some comfort, and I will offer prayers for your well being.'

"'Don't give him that. You don't need to give him anything,' said the woman. 'It is true, Lord,' said the leper, 'give it to the poor, who really need it.' The trapped man began to cry as he took the leper's hand and kissed it. 'You are the kindest of men with a good heart. Why is it you have to suffer so, while there are others with cold hearts who do not seem to suffer?' he said, looking at his companions.

"The leper replied, 'Sometimes it is a little suffering that opens your heart to others. Sometimes suffering can be a gift as it fills your heart with love and compassion. Sometimes suffering brings you closer to God, who, in His mercy, will reward those who suffer with His eternal love in Heaven.'"

"Children, do you understand this story?"

"Yes, yes, we do," they shouted.

Then one said, "It is the goodness in your heart that counts, not what you look like."

"That is right, My child, but also it says, sometimes you may suffer in life and this can be a gift, if through it all you can love," I said. Then we made our farewells and left.

J
E
J E S U S
U
S

Jesus ††† 6-12-96

Walking from Nazareth I still had thoughts of My Mother with Me, thoughts of My childhood days, thoughts of family life, thoughts of happy days. Judas (not Iscariot) came to Me asking, "Where do we go to now, Master?"

"Wherever My Father wills it," I replied.

"Don't You have any plans or concerns about where we go and why?" he queried.

"I leave it to My Father. He will guide Me to where He wishes Me to be. He will lead Me to what He asks of Me, and He will show Me what I must do."

"Lord, I am amazed at how you can trust so. I would find it difficult to be like that," Judas said.

"But you follow Me now without doubting. You follow wherever I go, and you trust that I will lead you along the right path. So you see, you do it already without knowing. You trust and have faith in Me, but you do not understand it. This shows true faith because it comes from your heart without doubt, without proudly proclaiming how strong your faith is. It is there, it is strong, and it is plain for all to see, except yourself. This is how faith is," I replied.

"Lord, I follow You because I love You and I know You speak from the Father. How could I not follow You?" He stated it, as if it was a fact that was obvious.

"Many will know, like you, that I am with the Father, many will profess to love Me, and many will listen to My words. However, unlike you, many will not have the faith that gives trust in Me; many will not follow where I wish to lead them, and many will even deny My love for them, and their love for Me. Judas, My friend, you are strong in your heart and pure in your love. Never change," I said, as Peter came forward and started to discuss the events at Nazareth.

J
e
J e s u s
u
s

69.

Jesus ††† 6-15-96

Evening fell as we approached a village that I had visited as a child. The lights from the houses shone like stars in the sky. They were beacons guiding us to the safety of the village...lights shining in the dark illuminating the way and guiding us home...light giving protection from the dark, bringing warmth and security. Why would anyone leave the light?

We entered the village and went to the inn to find a place to stay. Bartholomew and James came to me whispering, "Master, there are many drunkards here, many violent men. Maybe we should go from here?"

James added, "It is a little frightening here, Lord, should we leave?"

"It is where confusion and sin reign that we need to be, for these are the ones who need the most help. What good is it speaking to those who believe, if we ignore the others? I come to save all mankind not only a few. I offer forgiveness and love to all. They only need to accept it. To accept, they must first know what is offered, and in times to come, this will be yours' and all of My followers' work for Me," I said, in quiet reply.

We sat at a table for a meal. All around us was the noise of people who thought they were enjoying themselves by drinking to excess and telling bawdy stories.

"Master," said Peter, "isn't it sad how many seek comfort in wine, when they could find true comfort in God?"

"What do you mean?" shouted a man at the table behind us. "Who are you to criticize us?" he said, as he stood up, looking angry and ready to fight.

Peter stood up. "I did not mean to offend you, my friend, please forgive me," he said.

"Forgive you?" boomed the other. "You sit here and criticize, and on top of that you are a coward!"

"I mean you no offense. We are only here to rest and eat. Please do not be upset," said Peter.

"A coward who has no backbone," replied the man as he pushed Peter. I saw Peter's face becoming red and I knew he would lose his temper at any moment.

"Peter, sit down," I said softly, as I stood up next to him.

"Do You want to fight?" said the man.

"No, I do not want to fight you, I only want to help you. I see your struggle within, how you need to be angry to prove yourself. How as a child, your father always loved your brother more than you, and so now you try to prove you are a strong man, worthy of your father's love."

I reached forward and placed My hand on his shoulder, as he stood there confused. "I love you, and your true Father in Heaven loves you. Find peace in God, My friend," I said. He staggered for a moment then sat down in a daze, as Peter said through the silence, "Is he all right?"

"Yes, he is just letting go of some pain now. Then he will be fine," I said. We continued with our meal in almost complete silence, until the man came to his senses. He had sobered up and there was a sparkle in his eye. He spoke, looking directly at Me, "Can I sit with You for awhile, Lord?"

"Of course you can, My friend," I replied. Within a short time, he had become the best of friends with Peter. He kept apologizing to Peter, "I am sorry, forgive me. I don't know why I was like that."

"Of course I forgive you," said Peter, "it was nothing." Then Peter put his arm around the man smiling happily. "Lord," said the man to Me, "can I come with You when You leave?"

"What of your wife, your children, your father... what of them?" I answered.

"I will leave it all for You, I can't understand it, but I love You," he said.

"If you love Me, stay with your family and love them. In this way, you show your love for Me. The love in a family is God-given, so treasure it. Show it to the world, and in this way spread God's love," I said.

"But I so want to come with You, Lord. I want to be with You always!" he said, sadly.

"I am with you always. For the rest of your life, I will be in your heart and by your side. Never be lonely...never be lost. Know I am there, and tell others of Me. This is your way of following Me." I replied.

The rest of the evening was spent happily discussing God's love and God's will in peoples' lives. Before the man left he said, "I go now, Lord, to start a new life. I feel refreshed, strengthened. It is wonderful. If You ever need me, Lord, just ask, and I will be there."

"You will be needed in the future to stand and proclaim the mercy of God and I know you will do it well. Live your life for God and go in peace." We all said our farewells to him, and as he was leaving, Peter said, "By the way, what's your name?"

"Joseph," he replied.

"That is a good name for a man of God," said Peter, looking at Me.

J
e
J e s u s
u
s

Jesus ††† 6-16-96

We went to our chamber to retire. It was a large room we were to share. Judas Iscariot said, "It will be crowded and uncomfortable here tonight. Master, maybe You, and some of us more senior followers, should have another room."

I looked at him and said, "Judas, you are all loved equally by Me, and I love being with you, even if it does mean some discomfort." Judas looked disappointed but turned to the others and said, "The Master must have the most comfortable place," as he looked around the room, pushing the others out of the way.

"Here, Lord, this is the best place, and I will sleep next to You to keep You warm in the cold night," he said.

"No, Judas, I will sleep here, it is suitable. Come and lie next to Me here," I replied.

"But, Master, that is the coldest part of the room. There will be a draft there," he said, with a worried look on his face.

"I do not mind, My friend, for I will have you next to Me to keep Me warm," I said, smiling softly at him.

With a lot of complaining, Judas came and lay beside Me. "It is much better over there, and that boy, James, is enjoying it. Look how happy he is," said Judas. I looked at James who looked so content, so peaceful, and so comfortable. I looked back at Judas and said, "Yes, it is good to see him so," and then I turned around and fell asleep.

I was woken in the middle of the night to see Judas trying to make James exchange places with him. James, half asleep, was protesting and rubbing his eyes. "Judas, I thought you wanted to be next to Me?" I said. Judas looked at Me, embarrassed that he had been caught in the act.

"I do, Master. I was just getting a warmer covering for You, as You looked cold. I thought I would give James my covering for his, and put it over You to keep You warmer," he said.

"To cover one's weaknesses does not hide them, and to hide them in deceit only makes them larger," I replied. "Leave James alone and return to your place, and pray to My Father that you can overcome your weaknesses or one day they may destroy your very soul," I said sadly, thinking of what was to come.

Judas returned and did not move again that night. I remained awake, seeing before Me in Judas, the weakness of so many others...so many who would not admit when they were wrong, and in their pride, cover up their sins with more sins, and then more sins to cover these. This is the way of sin and evil. It traps many, like Judas, into a spiral that drags them deeper and deeper into the dark. Poor Judas, so many weaknesses, and so blind he cannot see them.

J
E
J E S U S
U
S

73.

Jesus ††† 6-23-96

We rose and began to pray together, offering the day before us to the Father for His glory and asking His will to be done in our lives. James spoke up, "Lord, why do we have to keep offering our lives over and over to God? Surely once is enough."

"My friend, we offer our lives to the Father each day to remind us that we are living for, and by, God's will. When you were a young child," I said, as Judas cut in, "He still is, he still is, Lord," laughing at his humor, while everyone else was silent.

James responded quickly, "I may be young, but at least I do not complain all the time, or keep for myself what is to be shared."

"James, do not get angry," I said, "To be a man of God means to control your anger, and to control your tongue. As for you, Judas, do not make fun of others as this is a sin. Humor does not mean belittling others. Humor should be joyful and humor should never hurt."

Judas, looking downhearted, said, "I am sorry, Lord. I won't do it again." But I knew he would.

I continued, "Now, not only James, but all of you, listen. When you were children, how many times did you tell your mother and father you loved them? Didn't each time make them happy? How many times did your parents say they loved you? No matter how many times they said it, you wanted to hear it, because it brought you joy, comfort, and security.

"It is the same with the Father. He waits to hear your words of love, and He listens to each one. No matter how many times you tell Him you love Him, He listens and enjoys it. Then the Father returns His love to you in joy that brings you comfort and security, for then you know in His love nothing can harm you.

"So understand that it is good to offer every day to the Father in love because it brings great joy to Him. Also it brings comfort and security to you, knowing that each second is God's, and that God is with you throughout the day."

"Let us praise God some more," said Matthew excitedly.

"Let us open our hearts to Yahweh," said John in agreement.

Simon started to pray out loud, "Father, I love You, I love You, I love You." Soon everyone was praising God joyfully, except Judas, who looked as if he wanted to be elsewhere.

While we ate our morning meal, a servant came to me and asked, "Is it true, Lord, You are Jesus the Nazarene?"

"Yes," I said softly, looking into her eyes. She continued, "Oh Lord, I had heard so much about You, and someone said You had come to free the captives. Please free me, Lord, I so want to return to my family in Samaria, but they owe a debt to the owner and I must work here until it is repaid. I don't like it here. The men touch me and make fun of me. I want to go home. Please help me, Lord, I am so ashamed of what I have to do here. Please help me or I will die," she said, as she fell to her knees with her head in her hands crying.

I reached out and stroked her hair. "My child, I know you hurt inside. I know you are often forced to do what you do not want to do. I know others make you feel worthless, as if you are nothing and only there for their convenience.

"Well, My child, you are beautiful within as well as without, and I truly love you. Do not think of what you do as your sins, for you are forced to accept what others do to you. I know you reject what is asked of you, so how can it be you who commits the sins? If another puts his will upon you and you cannot stop it, then how can you sin?

"Do not despair. To take your own life is not the answer. All that will accomplish is to bring pain and guilt to your family, who already have broken hearts at what is demanded of you because of their debt. Your father loves you, and the shame you have seen in his eyes is not because he is ashamed of you, but because he is ashamed of himself, that his daughter has to do this because of his debts."

She looked at Me with big eyes from which tears were flooding out. "Do you think my father still loves me? Does he really, Lord?" she said.

"Of course he does, and you must love and forgive him," I replied. She was still kneeling and looking at Me when the owner came to us. "Stop crying, girl. Get on with your work and do not bother the guests," he barked at her.

"It is all right," I said, "I am happy to talk to her."

"She is worthless, Master. She is lazy and will find any way not to do her work," he said, in an accusing manner.

"Would your daughter like the work you force upon this child?" I answered, looking directly at him.

"N-N-No, she wouldn't. But my daughter is a sweet child, not like her," he said, pointing to the girl.

"And what makes your daughter any different from her?" I asked.

"Well, this girl is a Samaritan and her father is in my debt," he replied quickly.

"So because of this, she is worthless?" I asked.

"The debt must be paid and she is the payment. I would never give my daughter as payment for a debt. That proves her worth. This one, though, cannot be very good, because her father gives her away," he stated vehemently.

"But he was forced by you, with the threat of imprisonment," shouted the girl.

"Be quiet, girl," he said, as he raised his hand to hit her.

"Stop!" I said, "Do not strike her. How much is the debt?" I said, as Judas began to look nervous.

"Ten silver pieces," he replied.

"It's not that much," said the girl. "It was only two."

"Shut up or I will beat you," shouted the man. Anyway there is the interest to consider." I looked into his heart and could see greed, anger, hate, and darkness. Then I started to cry a little.

"What are You crying for?" asked the owner, "Does a little thing like her affect You so?"

"I am crying for you, My friend, for I see only sadness and darkness in your soul. I see the man you killed in a jealous rage, and I see the price you will have to pay for your sins when you come before God," I said, sadly.

"God! Who is He? Who cares? Will you pay her debt or not?" he demanded.

"Judas," I said, "pay him." The owner looked happy while Judas looked sad as he handed over the money. I looked at the girl and said, "Go to your family and love them." She ran forward and put her arms around My neck and kissed My forehead many times saying, "Thank You, thank You, thank You." The owner counting his money said, "What a waste of money."

"No," I said, "what a waste of a soul."

The girl collected her few belongings and came to Me before she left saying, "I will never forget You Lord."

I said, "Nor I, you. Remember, do not be ashamed for you have done nothing to be ashamed of, and know that God loves you." She left singing a Psalm and skipping as she ran along the road.

"Let us go," I said. "I do not wish to stay here any more."

"But you haven't finished your meal," said the owner.

"I no longer have an appetite for it," I said.

We walked to the synagogue, and along the way Bartholomew and Peter were beside me. Bartholomew was talking about the events at the inn. "I sometimes wonder, Lord, how men can be so blind. Doesn't that man know what he is doing to himself?" he asked.

"Yes, Lord, I wonder at that also. Surely that man knows in his heart that what he did to that girl and her family was wrong, and that he was living against God's law," said Peter. "When he was about to hit that girl, I felt angry within, and I think I would have beaten him if he had not stopped when You asked him," he added.

"You see, my friends, how sin is? How it changes hearts, and how the sins of another may cause you to sin? That poor man, for he is poor in spirit, has allowed sin to cover his heart. Long ago he used to feel guilty at his evil ways, but he did not listen to his conscience. Instead he hid his feelings, and in doing this, accepted more sin into his life. Eventually his conscience became so hidden, he cannot hear it. With no conscience to guide him, sin no longer seems evil, so he accepts more and more. Then he sees it as the normal way to be. When he hurts others it seems as nothing, for now he has no feelings. When he sees others weak before him, he takes advantage of them and uses them as his belongings. This is truly evil. Greed covers his heart, pride fills his soul. The evil one stands at his side, but he cannot see it.

"This is spiritual blindness, a blindness worse than the physically blind, for even a blind man knows he is blind, but those with the spiritual sickness often do not know it. The evil within and around people like this then reaches out to others, trying to drag them into it's web of malice. Sometimes when others become angry with what they see in a man like this, they often start to resent or even hate him. They want to prevent his evil, even if it means sinning themselves...maybe in violence, maybe in hateful persecution, or maybe in a spreading of resentment among others. These people are themselves becoming blind to the evil that is now entering their hearts, because they believe what they do is for good. If this path is taken and not seen for what it is and to where it leads, then that is how evil can turn good people into bad without them knowing it.

"Never doubt that the evil one is clever in his deceit. And always, yes always, in everything you do, say, or think, remember to bring love and peace to the front."

As I finished speaking, Bartholomew replied, "Lord that is so true. I see it clearly now. I also was feeling angry towards the owner and wished him harm. Now I see I should have been praying for him, for he needs to be healed of his spiritual sickness so badly."

"Yes, Lord, I am sorry, too, for feeling so angry. I was going to hit him when I should have been praying for him. I feel ashamed of myself, Lord," said Peter.

"Do not be ashamed, be happy that you now can see how evil tries to trap you, and be happy that in your love, you now want to pray for this poor man, who truly is blind," I said, as we reached the synagogue.

J
E
J E S U S
U
S

Jesus ††† 6-24-96

We entered the synagogue and began to pray. Then after awhile I stood up and said, "David, a man filled with faith and love of Yahweh, set before a nation the example of the power of God's love. David's seed lives on in the nation of Israel, but does the inheritance of faith survive? Today I wonder what David would say if he saw his descendants, and the way in which they love and trust in God.

"Would David be ashamed of what he sees? Would David be saddened by the sin that abounds today? Would David say, 'Is this my family? Are these my descendants?' Would David wonder how what he had won for God, with God, and through God, had been given away so easily? Would David condemn the generation of today?"

As I finished, an old man named Thomas, whom I had known in my youth, stood up and said, "You speak well, Jesus. You give us much to think about, and You show us a wonderful wisdom in one so young. How I wish more of today's young men were like You. What You say makes me think about so many of the young today, who are only interested in themselves, and spend little time in the synagogues. I often think of them as a lost generation.

"Then I look at many of the elders and see why the young are as they are. I look at the leaders in the land, so many of whom think only of their power, their wealth. They bow before false gods and accept the will of foreigners and disbelievers into their faith. They appease others so that they can keep their positions of power and influence. You are right, Jesus. David would wonder what has happened to this nation, the nation of Yahweh."

Then he sat quietly as everyone in the synagogue pondered My words and Thomas' reply. On leaving, Thomas came to me outside. "Jesus, my boy, it is good to see You again," he said.

"And it is good to see you again, Thomas," I replied.

"You know, Jesus, You still make many of the people in the synagogue angry with Your words!" He smiled as he spoke.

"Yes, I know, but the truth must be spoken so that the people can be shaken from their slumber," I said, in answer.

"Jesus, I always see the wisdom in Your words, but many do not. Take care, for they may seek to harm You," he said, with concern showing on his face.

"I must speak the truth and speak of God's love, for there is nothing else. God is all," I said.

"I know, I know, but just take care Your zeal doesn't get You into trouble, my boy," said Thomas. "Will You come to my house for awhile so we can talk?" he asked.

"Of course I will. I always enjoy talking to you," I said, thinking of past conversations we'd had.

His home was neat and tidy, but you could see it was the house of a lonely man.

"Jesus, You know most of the people here think I am going mad with old age. When I ask them to turn to God more in their lives, most ignore me or make fun of me. They think since my wife died that I have become difficult," he said, looking a little sad.

"If you are mad, My friend, then it would be good if all were that way, for the madness they would have, would save their souls," I smiled.

We spent most of the day with Thomas, and My disciples were amazed with the depth of his love for God and the wisdom in his words. When we were leaving he said to My followers, "Listen to Jesus, for from when He was young, I have known Him, and I have known that God is with Him."

I reached out and took his hand saying, "Farewell, Thomas, and God has His hand in yours, too." He looked at Me and his face shone as he came to understand what I had said. I knew he would never be lonely again.

J
e
J e s u s
u
s

Jesus ††† 6-26-96

"Let us leave tonight," I said, no longer wishing to stay in this town. "It is time to go to Jerusalem. We shall start tonight on the journey."

"But, Lord, it will soon be dark and we should rest," said Judas, anxiously.

"My friends, we have rested most of the day. It will do no harm to walk for some of the night," I said out loud to no one in particular. I looked and saw it was not only Judas who was unhappy, for some of My disciples did not like to travel at night.

"It could be dangerous, Lord," said Bartholomew, who always preferred to sleep at night, and often at other times as well.

"We have nothing to fear, for the Father watches over us," I replied.

Peter who usually was supportive spoke up, "Master. I think it would be wise to wait until the morning. There are many dangers traveling at night."

"Peter, do you trust Me?" I asked.

"Of course I do, but we must be sensible," he answered.

"Peter, do you trust Me?" I asked again.

"You know I do, but this could be dangerous," he answered.

"Peter. do you trust Me?" I asked again, looking directly at him.

"Yes, Lord, I do, and I will do whatever You ask," he said, with a defeated look on his face.

"Trust," I said, "is when nothing blocks your acceptance that you are safe in My arms, safe with the Father, and safe by the Holy Spirit. Trust is a complete abandonment to the will of God, regardless of what dangers may arise. For when you trust, you know in your heart that God will protect you."

James interrupted, "I trust You, Lord, but am still a little afraid of what may lay ahead."

"It is natural to be afraid at times, but it is when you overcome these fears by trusting that God will look after you, that you show true faith," I said to all of them.

We collected our belongings from the inn where we had left them. When the owner saw us leaving he shouted out, "Going to free some more servants?" and he started to laugh. Peter had reached the breaking point with what had happened with the girl, and now having to walk through the night was the last straw. He rushed at the owner and was about to place his hands on the owner's neck.

"Peter!" I said, sharply. "Stop it! That is not the way." Peter stopped suddenly realizing that he had allowed his temper to get hold of him. Peter turned and started to walk back towards us, as the owner called out after him, "Typical of a coward. He shows false bravado when he knows his friends will stop him." He then started to laugh loudly, as did many at the inn. Peter was now feeling very ashamed because of all the taunts so, as he came to Me, I said, "My friend, I know it is difficult to ignore these taunts but when you do, you show your deep love of Me."

"Lord," said Peter, "it is very hard at times."

As we walked from the inn we could still hear the laughter. I said to Peter, "You are a courageous man, for it took a big heart and a strong spirit to act as you just did. You make Me very happy, My friend."

Peter, still hurt, replied, "Lord, to walk the path of God with You is very frustrating at times."

"I know, My friend, but know that I am always there for you. Just ask for My help and it is yours," I answered, softly. All of a sudden James, John, and Andrew were at Peter's side. James took Peter's bag and said, "I'll carry that for you."

Andrew said, "Brother, I am proud of you. You didn't fight. You were an example to all of us on obedience and humility."

"Really?" said Peter, as he seemed to stand a little straighter. John spoke up, "Peter, I do admire how you can see in a moment, where you are making mistakes and then put them right. I have a lot to learn from you!"

Peter now had almost forgotten his embarrassment and said, "Come on then, let's go to Jerusalem."

Judas came to me and whispered, "Master, we must get some more money, for even the secret reserve I have is almost gone, what with the gifts, and paying to free the girl."

"Do not worry, the Father will supply all we need," I said. "I wonder, though, how many reserves you truly have?" I queried.

Judas, who left Me quickly, did not speak to Me again that night.

J
e
J e s u s
u
s

Jesus ††† 6-27-96

Dawn broke as we walked along the road, and the most beautiful colors formed in the sky as the sun began to rise.

"Oh Lord, look how glorious the dawn is," said John, as he smiled at the beauty before him. "God's creation for mankind to enjoy," he continued.

"Yes, John, My friend, but you should try to see the beauty in all of creation. The ant on the ground means little to many, but it is a creation of God, and it, too, is beautiful. Look at how tirelessly it works, how the ant can lift what it should not be able to, but it finds the strength, and how it works in union with its companions to achieve the tasks before it. What a wonderful creation of God, and given by God all it needs to fulfill its role in creation."

"Lord, I also see the message there for mankind to work together for the good of all. One ought never give up trust in God, for He will supply all that is needed for mankind to achieve his role in creation. And, that God is not limited in what He gives, for He can give more than mankind believes is possible," replied John.

"I wish all could see as you, John," I said, sadly.

"Lord, I will do whatever I can to teach them, if You will first teach me," John said, trying to cheer Me.

"I know you will, My friend. I know you will," I said, as we continued to walk.

83.

"Let us stop and pray for awhile," I said out loud. Everyone looked happy with that, as I could see they were a little tired. We gathered together under a large tree and began to recite some Psalms. Then we all sat in silent prayer for awhile.

Later, I said, "Let us sing a song to the Father, and then I will spend some time alone."

Our voices made sweet music in the morning air, as we praised God from our hearts. When we finished singing I left them, heading for a hill in the distance. I knew that John and James were following Me at a distance. They wanted to keep watch to make sure no harm came to Me. It was their secret, but I knew.

I came to the hill, which was green with the grass that covered it. Here and there were wildflowers which decorated the blanket of green with specks of color. How beautiful is creation! I sat quietly absorbing the wonder of all that My Father had created, and then I began to drift into gentle prayer. As I prayed, two angels appeared and knelt in front of Me. They looked to the ground in humility and in love. Then between the two angels was My Father.

"My Son, it will soon be time for You to stand high among men. The time comes when You must be strong, and victory will be Yours. Ahead of You now lies great trials, but as My Son, I know You will overcome them."

"Father, I know what You ask of Me and what I must do, but sometimes it seems so much that I do not know how I will persevere," I replied.

"You will, My Son. It is Your human self that brings these thoughts to mind. Know You have all of Heaven at Your command and by Your side. Then know You will have the strength of spirit to overcome, for Your Spirit is My Spirit, and as You are One with Me, nothing can defeat You."

Father's words filled Me, and already I felt the strength of His love within.

"Father," I said, "there is so much sin in the world and so much to come. When I see this, My heart nearly breaks to see how mankind tortures itself, and how blind mankind is to its predicament."

"Jesus, You are here to open their eyes and their hearts. You are here because We love mankind so much. We want to save them. You are here to show mankind that I do exist, and that through following Your words and Your actions, mankind will find the way to Heaven, the only way."

The words of My Father overwhelmed Me with the power of His love, and as I felt this, Father said, "You are the power of My love, and You are My love."

I closed My eyes and slept peacefully for awhile. Then I woke to the smell of bread being cooked, and I realized that I was hungry. Walking back to My disciples, who were busy cooking a meal, I saw James and John hiding behind a bush, still watching out for Me, still ever protective.

My friends were huddled around the fire, waiting for the bread to warm. Judas spoke up, "Lord, all we have is some warm bread to eat, and soon that will be gone. We need to get some money or we will starve."

"How many times have I told you Judas, not to worry? My Father will provide." I said, slightly disappointed that Judas would not listen to what he had been told many times. The others remained silent, just looking at the small amount of food we had between us. I knew they also wondered when the next meal would be.

"My friends," I said, cheerfully, "let us eat this and be on our way." There was not much response until James and John returned with their arms full of berries.

"Look," shouted James, as he opened his arms, and the berries fell everywhere.

"Just over there are bushes full of the tastiest berries," John joined in, "Yes, they are delicious; try some."

Soon everyone was happy as they ate the berries with the warm bread; it was a wonderful meal. I quietly thanked My Father, and then said, "God has given us in creation all we need. Let us thank My Father in prayer."

The disciples, now looking content after the meal, joined joyfully in praising God. When prayer was over I said, "If you trust in God completely, God will supply all you need and lift all of your concerns. It just takes trust."

They looked at Me in agreement, but I knew for some, it was an agreement given only when they are happy, not when they are sad.

We continued our journey, and as we came to the next town, a large crowd came to greet us, shouting, "It is Jesus. He is here." Many were calling out, "Jesus, touch me. Jesus, heal me."

As they milled around us, I could just see some beggars who were blind, mute, or crippled, leaning against a wall. I turned and walked towards them, with voices shouting, "Heal me, Jesus, heal me," and hands reaching out to touch Me. My disciples struggled to keep order.

I came to the beggars, some of whom were not even aware I was there. I looked and saw they were in a poor condition, with their clothes torn and their bodies thin from hunger. Obviously, the townspeople did not care too much for the less fortunate.

I leaned over a young man huddled on the ground. He was blind, deaf, and dumb. His face was full of fear because of past abuse and rejection from others. As I looked into his soul I saw the pain, the loneliness, the despair. And, then I saw all of mankind within this man. I reached out and placed My hands on his head, saying gently, "My Father, I bring Your love to heal this child before You, and to glorify Your name."

The young man opened his eyes and then said. "I can see. I can see, I can speak. Yes, I can speak, and I can hear my voice. Praise God, praise God!" He started to dance around, as the crowd looked on in amazement. Then to their surprise, the other three beggars shouted,

"I can walk!"

"And I can see!"

Then all four started to dance and sing, praising God. The crowd was silent for a moment. Then they all started to shout, "Heal me, touch me." I walked among them, touching many and healing many. Later as I had almost finished with the people, I saw Judas among them collecting the coins they offered. He looked very happy.

J
E
J E S U S
U
S

Jesus ††† 6-29-96

"Let us find a place to rest," said Peter. You must be tired Master, for the people ask so much of You." As I was about to reply, a woman who had been following us for some time, but had stayed in the background, came forward.

"Lord, I would be happy if You and Your disciples stayed the night at my home," she said, looking hopefully at Me. "There is plenty of room."

"Don't stay with her," shouted some of the people, who remained after the crowds had gone.

"She made money by giving herself to a Roman. We have little to do with her. She is tainted," they said, with scorn in their voices. I looked at her and saw a tortured heart within, such pain, such sorrow, and yes, so much love. She turned to leave fearing the usual rejection she attracted from her neighbors.

"Of course we will stay with you," I said. She stopped suddenly and spun around saying, with surprise in her voice, "You will!"

"Yes, I will be happy to," I replied, looking at the people who were now silent, but who were glancing at each other in disbelief.

"I do not live far if You would follow me," she said bewildered. Walking to her house Matthew and Judas (not Iscariot) both spoke to Me. Matthew first, saying, "Is this wise Master, it may upset the townspeople?"

Then Judas said, "Yes, Lord, we do not want to cause trouble or get a bad name."

"If after all this time following Me, you are still worried about the thoughts of others, then you have not been listening to all that I have been teaching you. There is no judge of people except God, and when mankind tries to judge, often it is with malice or hate. Never judge others. Leave that to

God. Only see in others the chance to help them, the chance to bring them closer to God. If you do anything else, then you do not do My will, you do man's will. Try to remember God is the only judge, and it does not matter what others think of you. Please God in your life, not man. You cannot do both without compromising your service for God, so always put God first," I said.

Matthew replied, "Lord, we are so weak. It is so easy to give in to the pressures others put upon us. It is so easy to return to thinking with our heads instead of our hearts. Forgive us, Lord, and help us to understand better, so we can be more like You."

"One day, My friend, that understanding will come into your heart. One day your spirit will be set on fire with the Spirit of God that will fill you with compassion and love. One day you will know all that you search for now, but find so elusive. That day will be a day the world will remember," I said, thinking of a room filled with My disciples and My Mother, a room that would be filled with love.

Matthew and Judas looked at Me puzzled; they did not know I was talking of an event in the future that would anoint them with the Holy Spirit.

J
E
J E S U S
U
S

Jesus ††† 6-30-96

We arrived at the woman's house. On the way she had told Me her name was Judith, but she did not say much more. Her home was a very large house with high walls. At the door to greet her were two servant girls who guided us in, as Judith said, "Please make yourselves comfortable. My house is your house."

We entered a large room and My disciples began handing their few belongings to the servants, all except Judas Iscariot who would not let go of his bag, because it contained the donations we had been given.

Judith left the room and I could hear her with the servants in the kitchen saying, "Prepare the best food we have, and bring the finest wine. Do your best as we have a special visitor, and I want to please Him."

One of the girls replied, "But you know our food is little now, and soon you will have to sell something else to pay your bills. What shall we give them? We only have some bread and some milk. We have no wine."

In a kind but slightly worried voice, Judith said, "Here, child, take this ring and sell it. Then buy the best wine and the best food you can find."

"It is your wedding ring. You cannot sell it," said the other servant girl in surprise.

"It is only a ring," said Judith, with a sadness in her voice. "The love I have for my husband, and he for me, still remains. Go on, sell it and bring food quickly. They must be hungry."

"Judith," I called from the large room. Within a few seconds she came hurrying into the room with her two servant girls beside her.

"Yes, Lord," she said nervously.

"Judith," I said again, looking at her lovely gentle face, "My disciples and I had a wonderful meal this morning, so tonight we would be happy just to have some bread and milk, if you would have that."

"But, Lord," started to say Judas; he stopped when Peter elbowed him in the side.

"Are you sure, Lord Jesus?" said Judith, a little confused. "You must be very hungry after all the time You spent with the people today."

"Judith, bread and milk will do, and not too much of it. What I need more than food is to rest. Maybe, though, you would walk with Me in the lovely garden I saw as we came in." She turned to the servant girls and said, "Girls, bring the bread and milk as the Lord asks, but warm it a little first." Both servants turned and went to the kitchen again.

"Let us go to the garden," I said, as I slowly began to walk to the door. The beautiful fragrance of flowers filled the air; it was a perfume of My Father's creation.

"Judith, I know you are troubled. Can I help you?" I asked.

"No Lord, I am all right; do not concern Yourself with me. There are others who need You more than I," she replied, shyly.

"I am here to help everyone. No one is unimportant to Me, and no problem is too little or too large. Let me decide if you are worthy or not," I said, smiling softly at her, seeing in her many who judged themselves harshly, many who thought themselves unworthy when often they were the most worthy.

"Oh, Lord," she said, as we sat down on a bench. "My husband was a good man. Yes, he was a Roman, and yes, often he had to ask from the people what they did not want to give. He was a good man, Lord. He would give freely to the poor from his own pocket. He never turned anyone in need away, and he never kept any of the revenue demanded by Rome. Sometimes if people could not pay, he paid for them. He was so kind, so gentle, and he always seemed to know how to help and what to do in difficult circumstances.

"Last year he was killed by brigands as he went to Jerusalem. Well, then the soldiers came and took vengeance on the townspeople for his death. Now the same people my husband, Anthony, helped, have turned against me. They shun me, abuse me, and sometimes throw stones at me. Even the children mock me.

"Everyone in the town thinks I am wealthy, but apart from the house, I have nothing, for my husband gave most of what we had to them, when he was alive. Now even my son has had to go to my sister's home, for the children here beat him."

She started to cry as her heart opened with the thoughts of her husband and her son. "Lord, the only friends I have are my two loyal servants, and even they get abused. I wonder how much longer they will stay?" she sobbed.

"Judith," I said, as I placed My arm around her, "sometimes, when you lead a good life, so many bad things happen and you wonder why. Well, it is because you are good and evil tries to destroy you. It attacks your family, your friends, as well as yourself, for evil will do anything to stop good. Sometimes evil works in others without them seeing it. They become jealous, angry, spiteful.

"They forget all the help you may have given them, for their hearts are blinded by evil. I believe your husband was a good man, and I see in you a kind, gentle, loving soul. This is how all should be. I also share in the pain in your heart, from the loss of Anthony, your husband, your son having to leave, and the treatment you receive from your neighbors, but do not let this change you. Stay as you are, so beautiful within. Keep that beauty and you will find eternal peace in Heaven."

"What of my husband? He was not a Jew. Will Heaven be closed to him?" she cried.

"A good man is always welcomed in Heaven, be he Jew or gentile. Your husband had a love in his heart that he shared with all, a love that many Jews do not have. His good heart was a gift from God, a gift he did not waste, as many others do. Yes, he was a Roman; yes, he did not know Yahweh, but he lived as God wants all to live. He lived in love, love of fellow man, and love of creation.

"Look at the garden he planted, it is so beautiful. Did he not say to you, 'With such beauty in the world as these flowers, there must be a God of creation who loves us, for why else would He give us such joy?' So you see, he did know God."

Judith was amazed. As she sat upright, she said, "How did You know my husband said that? I was the only one here when he said it."

"I just know," I said, "as I know your life will get better." She looked at Me wondering what I meant.

We went back into the house. The bread and milk were on the table and so we sat down, then said a prayer, and began to eat what was before us.

Judas spoke up after we had finished, "Lord, I am so tired, I would like to sleep now."

Judith answered before I could speak, "Your beds are ready, you can sleep now, if you want to." I looked at the others in the room. They were tired also, from walking all night and then controlling the crowds.

"Yes, I am tired, too," I said.

I woke to the sound of birds singing in the garden, and the sweet scent of the flowers filling the house. Anthony had certainly planted the garden well, and in a position where the gentle morning breeze blew the perfume of the flowers into the house. I rose and wandered into the garden, where I closed My eyes and prayed to My Father. After some time, I heard My followers whispering, "Shall we disturb Him?"

"No, it is better to leave Him."

I stayed in the garden all morning and late into the afternoon. It was so peaceful and good to be alone with My Father. When I came back into the house only Peter, John, and James were there waiting for Me.

"Lord," said James, "You have been in the garden a long time."

"Yes, James, I was resting with My Father," I replied.

"Oh," said James, uncertainly.

Peter spoke, "Do You wish to go to the synagogue now Lord?"

"Soon, Peter, but first I would like to speak to our host," I said. John answered quickly, "She has gone with the servant girls to sell some of her belongings in the market place."

"Let us go to the market place," I said. While we walked to the market, people began to follow us, some quietly, while others called out, "Jesus, touch me." By the time we arrived there a large crowd was around Me. Peter, James, and John were pushing them out of the way to make a path for Me. We came to where Judith and her servants were selling her goods. Judith looked at Me embarrassed, only saying, "Lord."

"Have you sold much?" I asked.

"Enough to buy some food," replied one of the servant girls.

"Judith, sell no more, keep the little you have," I said.

"But she has a big house!" shouted someone.

"Yes, she has plenty, she married a Roman!" shouted another.

I turned to the crowd, and said, "Yes, and how many of you did her husband help? You there, he gave you food when you had none. And you, he gave your wife clothes for your children. And you, he paid your taxes when you could not. He did so much for all of you, and look how you treat his widow. When he was alive, he helped the poor, and he was a Roman. Yet I saw yesterday the poor beggars, and how you Jews had treated them."

The crowd was silent with many of them looking to the ground. "You who proclaim to be God's chosen nation, often proclaim it with hardened hearts. God gave you hearts to love, yet I do not see them here. I see it in a Roman who has died, but a Roman who lived as God asks you all to live, in love."

There was a slight murmur in the crowd, then someone spoke up saying, "Yes, he was a good man. He helped me."

Then another, "And me, he bought my wife medicine when she was sick."

"He helped my child," shouted another. Soon many were telling of Anthony's good deeds in their lives. One man came and fell on his knees before Judith. "Your husband saved me from prison and a scourging. Please let me help you, however I can," he said.

Tears were pouring down Judith's cheeks as I raised My hands to silence the crowd, "Now you remember how good this man was. Treat his wife with love and respect, for it is no more than she deserves."

Soon many were coming to Judith and embracing her, asking for forgiveness. Judith was saying, "Yes, yes, of course," and smiling and crying at the same time.

I turned to Peter, John, and James saying, "Let us gather our friends and our belongings. It is time to move on, the healing has been done here."

We slipped away and found the rest of My disciples at Judith's house. Peter told them what had happened and then asked them to make ready to leave.

As we walked from the town, Bartholomew said, "It is a pity to leave. That bed was so comfortable." I smiled, thinking of how he liked to sleep.

"Master," said Simon, "will she be all right now?"

"Yes, she will. The blindness has been lifted from the hearts of her neighbors. Now she will be loved as she deserves," I replied.

Simon carried on, "It is strange how they forgot all the good things her husband did."

"It is their weakness within that allows them to be blinded by evil, a blindness that makes them unable to see good, a blindness that makes them respond in hate and anger, a blindness that comes from Satan, and a blindness that can be cured by love," I said, as we continued along the road.

J
e
J e s u s
u
s

Jesus ††† 7-1-96

Night was closing in as we walked on in prayer. Everyone was full of joy after the events in the town. Even Judas was happy with thoughts of the donations and gifts we had been given.

"It is time to rest," I said.

"Let us find a place to camp," Peter said out loud. "There is a bridge ahead, maybe there will be some cover there."

James started to run forward enthusiastically. "I will go and see," he shouted.

"He is always full of youthful energy," said Bartholomew.

"Not like someone I know," replied John, thinking of how easily Bartholomew could sleep.

Matthew spoke up, "Yes, and how much noise others make in their sleep," he said, looking at John, who often snored loudly.

James came running back. "Master, Master, it is perfect. There is no water, the river is dry. We can camp under the bridge," he said, happily.

Soon we had made a fire and settled around it. Judas gave Andrew some food to prepare, but Andrew did not want to cook. "I cooked last time. You do it, Judas!" he snapped, handing the food back to Judas.

"That's not right, I have been preparing the meals often. Someone else should do it," retorted Judas.

Within a few moments it had erupted into an argument between five or six of My followers. I looked to Peter and he nodded, then he stood up in the middle of them and said, "We will all go hungry if you keep arguing. I will cook tonight!"

The others quieted down as Peter laid some fish on the stones in the fire, which then began to sizzle and give off the appetizing aroma of fish cooking.

"Children do not squabble as much as you lot," said Peter, as he turned the fish. "Part of your learning to serve God is to be humble, even when you feel that you are doing too much because others do too little. You should accept this in humility and offer it to God as a prayer," instructed Peter.

I smiled as I knew he meant it, and I knew what an example of humility he would be to others in the future.

"Let us pray for the strength to be humble," said Peter. Together we joined in prayer to the Father and I was filled with joy at seeing Peter's humble but strong heart.

Later, as the others slept, I sat looking at the fire, praying to My Father. I could not sleep even though it was late. My mind was filled with thoughts of how easy it was for men to slip into sin. It only took a few words and an argument could begin. Sometimes these arguments filled the people with hate and anger, and often they could lead to violence. If only they could see that if they stopped these disagreements before they began, by being humble and loving, so much pain and sin could be avoided. Then slowly My eyes began to close, and I could feel welcome embrace of sleep.

As I opened My eyes, I saw that My disciples had already eaten and were collecting their belongings. James came over to Me. "You slept a long time. We have been awake for ages. We have eaten and said our morning prayers," he said.

"Yes, I must have been tired," I replied as I stretched My arms and stood up.

"Do not worry, Lord, I have saved You some food, and look, it is still warm," said James joyfully as he offered Me breakfast.

"Thank you, James, you are a good friend," I said, smiling softly at his innocent love. What a gift is his love. Peter came to Me as I ate. "We didn't want to disturb You, Lord, as we thought You needed to rest," he said.

"I did, My friend. I was more tired than I thought," I replied.

"Maybe, Lord, we should stay here today and just rest," said Peter, with concern.

"I think you are right, and it is peaceful here," I confirmed in reply. Everyone unpacked their belongings and began to make the area as comfortable as possible.

"I will go for a walk alone," I said out loud to all of them.

"Shouldn't You rest here if You are tired?" asked Matthew.

"I will rest with My Father for awhile," I said as I walked from them.

I had walked for about half an hour, with James and John discreetly following Me, when I came upon a beautiful green field with sheep quietly grazing on it. The smell of the grass filled My heart with joy and I lay down upon it to rest. While I lay there, sheep started to come closer and closer to Me and I could hear their bleating getting louder and louder.

Then My Father's voice filled My head, "Jesus, My Son, these sheep are like mankind. They want to get closer and closer to You, and they call louder and louder to You. Your presence, Your love, attracts them, and once they are close to You they do not want to leave. Mankind is the same. They cry out for God's love. They want to be closer to You. Your presence for many lights their hearts and brings peace into their lives, and once touched by Your love they never want to leave."

I looked at the sheep coming closer. Soon there were very many around Me, rubbing against Me as I stroked their heads. They were bleating louder and louder. Then, as I said, "Be quiet," they all became silent and lay down beside Me. I lay among the sheep feeling the softness of their wool, like a blanket around Me. All of a sudden a voice called out, "What are You doing among my father's sheep?" He was a young shepherd who was amazed to see Me lying with the sheep.

"I am resting," I replied.

"That's a funny place to rest. Don't you have a home?" he asked.

"This is My home," I said, as I rose and opened My arms to the world.

"I have never seen my sheep go to a stranger before. They usually run away," he stated, as a matter of fact.

"To them I am no stranger," I said, patting the heads of two sheep.

"It seems they like You and they are sensitive to people, so if they like You, You can't be bad," he said, as he reached out to take My hand.

"Have You eaten? I have some soup over at my camp. Come and eat with me," he offered.

"Thank you, My friend. It is good to see such a warm heart," I said, as we started to walk to his camp.

"How do You do that with the sheep?" he asked.

"The same way as you did with Me," I replied.

He was confused, so I said, "You opened your heart to Me in friendship, offering Me your food. Well, I opened My heart to the sheep, and offered them My love." His eyes grew larger as he laughed, "That's very clever. What's Your name?"

"Jesus," I said.

"Jesus, I am David of Bethsaida. My father owns these sheep and I, as the youngest son, must watch over them. But, I am not that young, for I am 22. My father puts me to look after the sheep because I will not marry, so I think he tries to punish me. It is no punishment at all for I love being alone. It gives me time to read Scripture and to think of God. Out here I see God in everything... in the animals, the plants, the sky, the rain, the sun... everything. God is good in all that He gives us," he said smiling, as he looked around.

"You are a wise man, David, for not many see as you do," I said to him, as I felt the joy in his heart, the joy of loving God.

"I wanted to be a priest but my father would not have it. He says I have my head in the clouds and I should be more concerned with raising a family and his business; but I cannot, I just want to learn more about God. Are You interested in God?" he asked, innocently.

"I am," I said. "I always was, and I always will be."

He looked at Me confused, and then said, "Here we are," as we reached his camp. "Sit down and we can talk." He offered Me a bowl of soup. It was made from vegetables and it was delicious.

"Tell me of Your thoughts on God," he said. "I am always interested in what others think."

"As you, I see God in all of creation. I see God's love in every creature, every plant, everything. I see God's love in every man and woman, and I see, with sadness, how many ignore, and sometimes even try to destroy, God's love," I said, before he cut in.

"My father's like that. He is a good man but he does not believe in God. Money and position are all he knows. It is sad."

"Yes, so many are like that, but those who love God must try to bring God's love to all. Just as you treasure all your sheep, even the ones who wander at times, God loves all his children, and God wants those who love Him, to help others to find His love also," I said.

"I know. That is why I wanted to be a priest, but Scripture says I must obey my father," he said, with a disappointment in his voice. "But at least out here, I have time to pray and read."

"My friend, have you truly opened your heart to your father and told him what you want to do?" I asked.

"No, I was too frightened," he said.

"Well, I tell you now, if you go to your father and speak from your heart, he will listen and grant your wishes, for he loves you, even though at times you may not see it. Remember when you fell into the well as a child, and how your father came down after you, and held you above the water for three hours until help came? How, even though his arms ached he would not let go of you, and how he handed you first to the rescuers with no thought for himself? This is the love your father has for you. Go to him. Talk to him, and your wish will be granted," I said.

He looked shocked, as he said, "How did You know that? Were You there?"

"No," I replied.

"How did You know then?"

"I know your whole life, and I know you will be happy from now on serving My Father in Heaven," I said, gently. He looked into My eyes and said, "Lord," as he fell to his knees.

"David, you are a true Son of God, and one day we will meet in Jerusalem where you will watch Me carry man's sins on My back, and you will wonder why I have to suffer so. Know that it is so all the sheep in this world will have a shepherd to follow. And know that I understand you will be unable to do anything to stop My suffering along the way," I said, thinking of the day I would carry My cross, and how David would be in the crowd, longing to help Me, but unable to.

"Lord," he said looking up, "I would do anything for You."

"Then bring as many people to love God as you can, and when you see My followers persecuted, help them," I said.

"I will, Lord, I promise," he said, truthfully. I knew he would, and I knew he would become a true follower of Mine, who himself would convert many to the way. I left him after finishing the soup and, as I walked across the field, he called out, "I am going to see my father today. Thank You, Lord."

By the time I returned to My disciples, it was mid-afternoon. Simon came up to me and said, "Did You have a good rest, Lord?"

I replied, "Yes, My friend, a very rewarding rest."

Just then James and John returned to the camp and tried to look inconspicuous. I said nothing until James, who could hold in his question no longer said, "I think You would meet many interesting people on such a long walk, Lord." John elbowed him and looked harshly at him.

"Yes, James, why today I met a shepherd who loves God, and one day will bring many souls into the light." James didn't say any more under a silent threat from John. "Today in a young man, I saw a wise heart and deep love of God. How I long for all to be like that." I sat down and closed My eyes, and quickly fell into a deep sleep.

J
e
J e s u s
u
s

Jesus ††† 7-2-96

I woke to a blazing fire which My disciples had made. It was evening and darkness had settled in. "Lord, You have slept a long time again," remarked James.

"It does not matter, James, how long the Lord sleeps. He obviously needs the rest," said Bartholomew, who was leaning back against a post of the bridge. "I often sleep," he carried on, "but afterwards I feel so refreshed. It is good to rest in sleep."

Everyone was looking at Bartholomew, knowing he had a deep relationship with sleep. "When I sleep, often I get the clearest of dreams which seem relevant to what I am doing in life, or what is about to happen," he said. Everyone waited to hear more.

"I keep having one dream, though, that I don't understand. I see a man on a cross. I can't see his face properly. All around him are angels singing the praises of God. Then a spear is placed into his side, and blood and water flow from the wound and flood the world. I don't know what it means, but I dream it often," he finished.

"Lord," said Simon, "can You tell us what it means?"

I looked at My friends and knew it was not time yet for them to understand, so I said, "It is a dream about the sacrifice that is needed to wash the world in God's mercy." Then I said, "I am hungry, is there any food?" I was handed some warm bread and wine mixed with water.

"It is a sacrifice that will be eternal," I said, as I broke the bread and began to eat; "a sacrifice that will save so many souls and open the gates of Heaven once more." I sipped the wine and water, "And, it will be offered over and over to mankind," I said. They all looked confused, and Bartholomew said, "I still don't understand, Lord?"

"You will one day, My friend," I replied, and finished the food. Then I rose saying I would like to walk alone for awhile.

As I walked, I thought of what I would have to give and why. I saw how many would accept or deny My offering, and how many would believe in the daily gift I would leave them after My death. My heart was heavy with these thoughts, when I heard James and John following Me. James had tripped over, and John was telling him to be quiet. It made Me smile within. What good friends they were, and how I loved them. Then I saw once again why I had to give. It was so that all mankind could be friends of God again.

I returned to the camp and it was late now. I had been walking for some hours and sitting on a wall just thinking of the path ahead.

Peter was telling a story: "And the men on the boat were so frightened. There were holes in the wood, and the boat was filling with water. Each of them was putting cloth into the holes trying to fill the gaps to stop the water gushing in, but to no avail. The captain of the ship said to abandon her, but there was only one small boat which would not hold them all. It was a boat which was used to take five or six men at a time to the shore, but there were eleven men on the ship. They could not all fit into the little boat; maybe it would hold eight without sinking."

"What did they do?" asked Thomas.

"Well," said Peter, "eight did get into the boat, and it didn't sink."

"What about the other three?" said Thomas.

"Before the eight got into the boat, they drew straws to see who would stay. The three who remained had lost."

"Yes, but what happened to them?" said Thomas, impatiently.

"I was coming to that," said Peter, indignant. "The three left behind began to pray to Yahweh for His help. As they prayed, the mast of the ship broke and fell before them. Seeing this they thought the end was near, until one said, "Let's tie ourselves to the mast and put it in the water, it will keep us afloat."

This they did, and the storm quieted as they entered the water. The mast kept them afloat for three hours until another boat came and rescued them."

"They must have been very frightened in the water all that time. I would have been," said Matthew.

"They were, I am sure," said Peter, "but do you see the wonderful way God saved them?"

"No, I don't," said Judas. "It was only because the mast broke that they were saved."

"Judas, it was God Who made that happen. When they were prepared to die for their friends, and they prayed for God's help, the three men thought God had not heard them. When the mast broke they thought it was the end. Then, in their moment of despair, the Lord showed them the way to safety. When they accepted it, God calmed the storm for them and brought a boat to their rescue. Do you not see in this story that God never deserts you? Sometimes you have to reach the depths of despair before it is time for God to save you, but He is always there offering help. You just have to accept it," Peter said.

Judas spoke up again, "When did they accept it?"

"When they tied themselves to the mast, and threw themselves into the sea at God's mercy," replied Peter.

"I still don't see it. I think it was luck," said Judas, sourly.

"Lord, You are back," said Peter, as he noticed Me sitting slightly behind him.

"Yes, Peter. That was a wonderful story you told," I said.

"It was true, Lord, it happened when I was young, and I always remembered it. My father told me of it," answered Peter.

"It is a story that teaches much, My friend," I said, softly, feeling happy inside at how Peter's knowledge of God's will was increasing. He will be an example to all and a teacher to all, I thought, as I lay back to sleep again. Just then James and John returned and I saw Peter nod at them. My friends, how I love them.

J
e
J e s u s
u
s

Jesus ††† 7-3-96

Morning broke and I had been awake for some time, just lying there feeling My Father's love filling Me. As the light shone in the sky from the rising sun, I arose and went to pray alone beside a large tree I had found the day before. Each prayer brought Me closer and closer to My Father. Then, before Me, I could see the throne of My Father where He was sitting looking at Me.

Father smiled and reached out with His hand, which touched My head, and I was united with My Father in body and in spirit. Our spirit united within Us and the Trinity of God was together in love. It only seemed as if a moment had passed, but in that moment I knew mankind from beginning to end, and I loved them, all of them.

When I finished praying some hours had passed, so I returned to My disciples who had collected everything and were waiting for Me so we could leave.

"Are You hungry?" asked Judas (not Iscariot).

"No, I think I will go without food today," I answered.

"You will need to eat for strength to walk," said Andrew, who was genuinely concerned with My welfare.

"I will be fine, My friend. Sometimes it is good to go without food," I replied, smiling at his love for Me.

"Then I am not eating again today, also," said James, loudly in his youthful zeal. All the others joined in agreeing, except Judas Iscariot, who kept quiet until everyone looked at him.

"I will not eat either, then," he said, looking very unhappy.

We walked until late in the evening. Through the day, I occasionally heard Judas saying, "Why do we have to go hungry. Whose idea was this? I'll kill that boy James." Judas liked his food and he wasn't happy to go without.

As night drew on, we stopped by the side of the road between some bushes which sheltered us from the wind and we lit a fire, which was so warm and welcome in the cool of the night.

"Will we eat now?" said Judas, hopefully.

I looked at him feeling sorry for the constant struggle he had within.

"You can eat if you want to, but I will eat in the morning," I said, softly, as I drew pictures in the ground with a short stick. The others spoke up,

"We will wait, also," they said.

"So will I, then," said Judas, defiantly.

"Sometimes," I said, "it is good to discipline your body. In fasting you can find the freeing of your spirit in prayer easier. Sometimes this discipline is needed to strengthen you for times when many difficulties face you, for when you discipline your body, you also discipline your mind. With a mind strengthened and under your control, it is easier to defeat evil when you face it. It is easier to overcome the bad times, and it is easier to sacrifice for others when you need to. See fasting as a grace not a punishment. When you do this, the days become a joy, not a torture, and the fast becomes another way of offering your prayers to the Father."

My disciples looked at Me in agreement. Judas even managed a smile, but I could see he was discretely chewing some bread he had hidden under his coat. Discipline seemed so hard for Judas to understand.

J
E
J E S U S
U
S

Jesus ††† 7-4-96

When I rose the next morning, I felt full of strength for the day's work ahead. I knew it would be a difficult day. My disciples ate a large morning meal. Judas seemed to have an appetite that could never be satisfied. I ate a little bread and did not need anything else. Then Judas with his mouth full of food said, "Jesus, You are not eating much, You will be hungry later," he warned.

"I have had enough," I replied, but he cut in before I could finish, spraying Me with the food from his mouth as he spoke.

"You may think that now, but wait until later in the day." He put more food in his mouth and drank some water. "I always make sure I have enough." How true I thought, even at the expense of others.

After the meal we went to a nearby well to draw some water to wash. There were two women there from a nearby farm.. When we came close to them, one young woman said, "Can I help you? Here, let me get you some water." She reached out to take our containers and began to fill them for us.

"Thank you for your kindness," I said, as I took the water container back from her.

"Yes, thank you," said My disciples, as each collected his water container from her.

"Where are you traveling to?" asked the other woman.

"Jerusalem," answered Peter.

"That is a long walk," said the young woman who had given us the water. "It will take you some time."

"It does not matter how long it takes," I said, "there is much we can do on the way." The older woman looked at Me, and said, "If You are in no hurry, maybe You could come to our farm. There is work there You could do. Our father is old and our brother cannot manage by himself. He has fallen behind planting the seeds, even with our help. We would feed You and pay You," she offered.

Peter spoke up, "We would like to help, but we must go to Jerusalem."

"It would only take two or three days, maybe less with all of you," said the younger woman, pleadingly.

"I think we can stay a while," I said, "but only for two days, no longer, for we have much to do."

"Thank You, thank You," said the two women in unison, looking very happy.

"Collect your belongings and follow us," said the older of the two. We returned to our camp. On the way Peter said, "Is this wise, Lord?"

"Peter, they need our help. We must never turn away anyone who asks for help," I answered.

"Yes, Lord," said Peter, obediently.

We collected our belongings and returned to the women, who were talking to each other.

Then the older said to us, "It will be good to have company. We don't see too many people on our farm because we are always busy working."

"Yes," joined in the other, "we don't even go to town that often."

James came up to the younger one, who was about his age. "You look as if you work so hard. You know, sometimes it is good to rest, for if you only work, life can become a burden," he said. I had to smile, for I saw in James someone who was beginning to learn what life's real meaning was.

The young girl smiled back at James, "That is easy to say, but when you have a sick father and a crippled brother, who can only do a little, life is a burden at times." James blushed for he did not know how to answer.

"Don't be embarrassed. Life is hard you know," said the older woman, gently, as she turned to lead us to the farm.

The walk to the farm was quiet. James seemed too frightened to say anything after the last time.

"Let us pray," I said, and so we all began to recite a prayer to the Father. Even the women joined in as we walked. When we finished praying, the younger woman said to James, "Are you holy men?"

"The Lord is," he said, looking at Me. "The rest of us are trying to be."

"Where do you come from, then? One of the big synagogues?" she asked.

"No," said James, "We come from different places, and we visit many different synagogues. Our Lord is a Rabbi," he stated, proudly.

"A Rabbi," said the older woman. "Maybe He can pray with my father and brother. They have not seen a Rabbi for a long time. With father sick and my brother, Michael, crippled, it is hard for them to go to the synagogue. I know they enjoy praying. Maybe later you could all pray with them?" she asked, hopefully.

"Of course we will," I said. "It will bring us great joy to pray with them."

We arrived at the farm and Michael came to meet his sisters. He hobbled as he walked and I could see both his legs had been crippled since birth, but he had enough strength to walk.

"Sisters," he called out, "you have brought so many visitors. Welcome, welcome," he said, smiling and laughing as he spoke. What a happy heart this man had through all his pain, and what a bright soul.

"I am Michael, let me help you with your bag," he said, as he half reached, half leaned, to take it.

"Thank you, Michael," I said, smiling back at him. "We have come to help you with your seeding."

"What a blessing from God you are," he said, happily, "God is good. You know, I was praying for help and here you are. Praise the God of Israel." He almost sang as he spoke, he was so happy.

Peter said, "Show us where to begin, then."

"Follow me, follow me. It is good you are so keen. There is so much to do," Michael said, as he led us towards the fields.

The younger sister looked at James, and said, "Thank you," quietly.

We spent all day working in the fields. During the day, the women brought us water to drink and food to eat. Michael worked so hard but could do so little because of his legs. All day he was happy and smiling, just so full of love. How I wished all men could be as Michael.

In Michael I saw a pure spirit filled with love, a love which covered the pain he felt within, from the mockery and abuse of others, from feeling less than a man, and from the pain in his legs every time he moved them. Through all this, his love shone through. Then I thought of those who, with little or no suffering, could not love anyone except themselves. What an example was Michael to them, if only they would open their eyes and look.

Evening was coming as we went to the house. We were washing the dirt of the work from us and feeling very tired, when Judas spoke, "See, Lord, I told You to eat more. You needed it today."

"Judas, I had plenty at the morning meal, and today there was the food the sisters brought to us. That was enough," I answered.

"Yes, Lord, that was good food," said Judas, thinking of what he had eaten out in the fields. "I can't wait for the evening meal."

We all looked at him in silence, until Peter threw a wet cloth at Judas, saying, "You are so greedy."

"What do you mean?" replied Judas, feeling hurt.

"I just have a good appetite. There is nothing wrong with that," he said, justifying himself.

"A good appetite is one thing," Andrew said, "but you are just greedy."

"That's not fair. I eat what I need to keep me going. I do a lot of work you know, more than most of you," Judas said. Thomas cut in, "Yes, counting all that money is difficult."

Judas looked to Me for help, so I said, "Let us go inside and join our hosts. Try not to argue, and I know tonight Judas will only eat a little, to show he is not so greedy."

Judas' chest expanded as he said, "The Lord is right, you will see. I am not greedy."

We entered the house after making sure we were cleansed of the dirt from the field. The older sister came to Me, asking, "Rabbi, will You pray with my father and brother first?"

"Of course we will," I replied. "Where are they?"

She led us all into a large room with a bed in the corner. In the bed was her father propped up by some pillows. Beside the bed, leaning against it, was Michael. When he saw us he said to his father, "Father, this is Jesus. He is a Rabbi who has been helping in the fields today with His followers." The older man smiled weakly at Me. "A Rabbi," he whispered. "Is it true?"

"Yes, My friend, it is," I said. His face seemed to brighten a little and he tried to sit straighter.

"Can we pray and read Scripture together," he asked. "It has been so long, that I think God may have forgotten me."

"God never forgets anyone. God knows every breath you take, every word you speak, every thought you have. To God everyone is special," I said, as the old man began to cry.

"But I have been unable to pray for so long. I can't seem to read Scripture. It is only when my son Michael reads to me, that I have God's words before me, and sometimes even then, I cannot hear Him. God must be so disappointed with me. Look at my poor son, a good, good boy with a big heart, but he cannot run the farm alone.

"My daughters never have time to visit, so they have no husbands. My family and I must be a shameful sight before God. I know I will die soon, but I am sorry that I have not made good with the gifts Yahweh has given in my family and in my land. Why, even my wife died from working too hard. I hope God will forgive me," he said.

"Old man, God loves you and will forgive your mistakes in your life. God has seen throughout your life how you love Him. God has heard all of your prayers, even when you thought you were not praying, for your thoughts of God were prayers. God looks upon your life and sees how, through difficult and very hard times, you never stopped loving Him. How even when your son, Michael, was born crippled, you and your wife thanked God for such a wonderful gift.

"God has seen how you loved your wife, and even when she died, you thanked God for her life, for the love she brought you every day she was with you, and for the love you could give to her. God looks upon your family and sees the pure love and joy in your son's heart, the generosity and kindness in your daughters, and the humility in their father, who loves God so much he worries that he can no longer go to the synagogue. What a man of God you are and what a family of God is your family," I said, as the old man began to cry from his heart.

"Oh, Yahweh, I do love You. Oh Lord, take me soon. Lord, please bless my family so they can be safe when I am gone." His arms were raised feebly in the air offering his words to My Father.

His voice trembled. "Rabbi, please pray with us and bless my family," he said to Me. Together My disciples, Michael, his father and I began to pray, as the daughters waited in the other room. I could see James crying in his prayers, and I felt by the prayers from his heart that My Father would help this family.

We prayed for almost two hours and as we finished the old man spoke, "Rabbi, thank You for Your prayers. My heart feels so happy now. Please bless my daughters before You go to sleep tonight."

"My friend, of course I will," I replied.

"Rabbi," he said, "how did You know so much about my life?"

"God knows all of your life," I said. He looked at me quizzically.

"But how did You know?" he asked.

"What the Father knows is known by the Son," I replied.

I could see he did not understand, then he said, "But who is the Son?"

"I am," I replied, leaving the room.

The older daughter came to Me, saying, "He will die soon, will he not?"

"Yes," I replied, "but he will die a happy death and leave behind a happy family." Both girls began crying softly. I placed My hands on their heads and said, "In the name of Yahweh, My Father, I bless you." With these words a calmness filled them and they set about preparing the meal. Michael came and sat next to Me at the large table in the room.

"Thank You, Rabbi Jesus, for praying with my father. I know he enjoyed it," he said.

"It is always a joy to be with a man who loves God," I replied.

Peter, who was sitting opposite Michael said, "I wonder, can anything be done for this good family?"

"We shall see," I said. "We shall see."

The dinner was delicious and there was so much food, but poor Judas sat with only a little on his plate picking at it and looking sad. James, who was next to Andrew was eating a large piece of meat on his plate and saying, "This food is wonderful." Judas looked at the meat with a hunger in his eyes. The younger woman, whose name was Elizabeth, said to Judas, "You are not eating much, have some more, there is plenty," as she put a dish of corn before him.

"I cannot," said Judas, "for tonight I have promised to eat only a little." I could see in his heart he wondered how he had made such a promise.

"But you must be so hungry after all the hard work in the fields," said Elizabeth, with concern in her voice.

"No, a promise is a promise," said Judas, as all at the table looked at him. I hoped Judas would learn from this, but I knew he would not.

After the meal we were so tired from the work most fell asleep quickly, but as I lay there thinking of My Father, I saw Judas crawl from under his blanket and go to the kitchen, to return moments later with some of the meat in his hand. Then the next few minutes were filled with chewing noises from where he lay, and then a belch before he fell asleep. Poor Judas could not find the strength to keep his word.

We rose early and spent some time in prayer with the old man. Then we went to the fields to finish the seeding.

"It should be complete tonight," said Michael, happily. "You all work so hard. You have done in two days what would have taken me weeks."

"Yes, tonight will be our last night here," I said, "and tonight will be a special time for all of us."

When we had finished the work, the seeding had been completed, and we all felt happy to have helped so. While washing, Judas was quiet, while the others were noisy in their joy of finishing the work. I knew Judas was being careful so he didn't have to make any more promises. Thomas said, "You are quiet, Judas, is anything wrong?"

"No," replied Judas, and he continued washing.

Entering the house the two women spoke to Me, "Will You pray with father again? He has been so happy since last night."

"We will," I said, "but tonight, I would like you both with us."

"That is not right," said Elizabeth. "You men should pray together, we will come in later."

"It is all right." I said, "Tonight is a special night, and I would like you to be with us."

"Are You sure?" said the older sister.

"Yes, I am," I said.

We all went into the large room where the old man was. Again he was propped up on pillows, and as I came towards him, he said, "I have been thinking on what You said last night. Is it true?"

"Yes," I answered. He began to smile and he spoke excitedly saying, "It's true," as tears ran down his face. "I can die a happy man now. I have seen Him."

Michael looked at Me confused. "What does he mean, Rabbi?"

"Michael, spend these last moments holding your father, and you as well," I said to the girls.

As they gathered around their father, he was touching their faces, saying, "We are blessed. He is here." Then his voice began to fade and he slipped into death's arms. Michael and his sisters began to cry. Then I came over to their father, blessed his body in death and began to pray. My disciples joined in the prayers. After praying, I placed My hands on the children and said, "Bring some oil, and we will anoint him. Then you must make him ready for burial."

All three stopped crying and were filled with peace. They did as I asked. When they had finished preparing the body, I said, "Let us go to the other room and celebrate this joyful moment, when your father's spirit has taken the final step home to God." In the other room was the food ready for the evening meal.

"I don't feel like eating," said Michael.

"Neither do I," said both of the women.

"Did you not see how happy your father was in death? But now you are sad. Do you think he would want you like this?" I said, gently, to them.

"No. You are right, he was happy wasn't he," said Elizabeth, forcing a smile and wiping a tear from her cheek with the back of her hand.

Soon we were saying the prayer over the food. Then we began to eat. Everyone was slow to eat, except Judas, who was wolfing the food down, saying, "This is delicious."

"Michael," I said, "you and your sisters should see the joy that is the truth of death. If like your father, you have lived a good life, a life for God, then death is a special blessing that will bring you to the Father and eternal happiness in Heaven.

"Death is not to be feared for it is only a step into the new life with God. Death brings the rewards of God's love to those who trust in God. Death is a wonderful gift from God."

"Yes, Rabbi, I know, but it is still a sad time," replied Michael.

"Sadness that is an expression of your love for your father, but you can also express that by accepting the happiness he saw in his death," I said, feeling the sorrow in their hearts.

"In the gift of death tonight, God also offers this family something else. Michael, go and see your father for a moment please." Michael rose and hobbled into the room; a few moments later he returned.

"I saw nothing, Rabbi," he said.

"Michael!" shouted his sisters together, "you are walking. You are walking."

Michael looked at his legs and saw they were straightened, then he ran around the room shouting, "I can walk properly! I can walk!"

The three of them then stopped, and said, "How can we be so happy? Father is dead."

I replied, "Wouldn't your father be happy to see his son so?"

"Yes, he would," they said, as they embraced each other crying with joy and with sorrow. My disciples began to sing a Psalm, thanking God for His mercy. All of a sudden Michael stopped embracing his sisters and with wide eyes fell before Me saying, "I understand what my father was saying now. I understand. You are the One. It is You, isn't it?"

I placed My hand on his head, and simply said, "Yes."

He began to kiss My feet and his sisters, who now also came to understand, joined him.

"My friends, there is no need for that. Be thankful to My Father in everything you do, and offer the love in your heart to others to help them come to the love of God," I said.

"We will Lord, we will!" they cried, in unison.

The next day we helped them bury their father but now there was only happiness in their hearts. Then, as we made our farewells, I said, "Keep your trust in God, and your lives will be full."

"Lord, You will come back, won't You?" said Elizabeth.

"I will be with you always," I said.

"But please, come back to see us," said Michael.

"I will, I promise," I said, knowing that the next time they would see Me would be after My resurrection, when I would come and visit them to show the truth of death, the truth that is eternal life. (Ref. Baruch 5:1, "Put off, O Jerusalem, the garment of thy mourning, and affliction, and put on the beauty and honor of that everlasting glory, which thou hast from God.")

J
e
J e s u s
u
s

Jesus ††† 7-5-96

When we left the farm I could see a little sadness in James' eyes. It was a sadness of leaving a good friend of the same age. James, I said. "Why not lead us in a prayer?"

"Me, Lord?" asked James, not expecting to be asked to lead prayers. "Shouldn't someone else do it?" he said, with a hopeful look now on his face.

"No, James, I would be happy if you could do it," I answered.

"Yes, Lord, if you want me to I will," he said, looking not so sad now. James began with a Psalm of God's mercy; soon everyone was joining in. When the Psalm finished, James began another, and when that had finished, another. James was really enjoying leading the prayers, and I saw My disciples were happy for him also. When the third Psalm was finished, James started to sing another, on the greatness of God. Some hours had passed before James stopped. Then he came to Me and said with joy filling his every word, "I enjoyed that Lord. I feel so wonderful, I could pray all day, but I don't know if the others would want to."

Peter, who was now walking beside Me, replied, "I would be happy to join you in prayer for the rest of the day. Prayer makes me feel good, too."

I smiled at the strength My disciples were finding in prayer, even though often they did not recognize it.

"Is it all right, Lord?" said James.

"Yes, My friend," I said, with a smile.

James turned to the others saying, "Jesus has said it is all right to pray all day, will you join me?" My followers were smiling at James with enthusiasm, as they agreed to his request. Even Judas seemed content. We spent the day in prayer, and as night fell we came to a town which was quite large, and so I said to Judas, "Please take Simon and find some rooms for us to stay." He smiled for he knew tonight at least he would be comfortable.

Judas and Simon returned after only a short while. "Master, we have found an inn with room for us all, and it is a reasonable price," smiled Judas.

"Yes, Lord," said Simon, "it is not far from here, and it appears to have room for us."

"Good, it is decided then, we will stay there," Peter said, loudly. I looked at Peter and saw how he was growing in his leadership abilities, and how the others were prepared to listen to him.

"Peter," I said, "it may be wise to see the inn first, and to find out what type of person owns it. Remember the last inn we stayed at, and that poor girl?"

Peter looked at Me, saying, "Yes, Lord. You are right as always. I will go and speak to the owner with Judas and Simon."

"But Lord, it is all right there," said Judas, with Simon nodding in agreement.

"Let Peter go with you, and if he has no objections, then we will stay there," I said.

Both Judas and Simon looked disappointed as if I didn't trust their word, so I said to them, "You did well finding an inn that has room for us all so quickly, but we do not want any more arguments like that over the food last time, or the mistreatment of the servant girl. Let us be a little more careful this time. It is wise to learn from what has happened in the past, so as not to make the same mistakes in the future. Sometimes just a little caution can save many problems."

The three of them returned to the inn, then a little while later they came running back to us as we waited at the outskirts of the town. "You were right to be cautious Master," said Simon, excitedly.

"There are Zealots staying there, and we heard they are planning to kill some Romans who are in the town," Peter joined in,

"They have many weapons with them and look vicious, Lord. We should stay elsewhere."

"My friends, if we turn away from those who are about to sin, without trying to help them stay on the right path, the path of goodness, why are we here? My Father in Heaven sent Me to overcome sin and so when we face it, we should not flee, but try to stop it," I said.

"But Lord!" cried Judas, nervously, "I do not think we can stop this. Those Zealots are so determined."

"Being afraid of standing against sin, only allows sin to grow. If you trust in God and stand firm in the truth, you have nothing to fear," I said. "Come on, let us go to this inn."

"But Lord, I thought you said to be cautious," said Simon, visibly shaken at the thought of facing the Zealots.

"To be cautious does not mean to hide from sin or to be afraid of it. To be cautious means not to do anything foolhardy, to be wise in your words and actions. With this wisdom also comes the knowledge of when to stand for what is right. This is true wisdom," I said, as I headed for the inn. "Being overly cautious is as bad as having no caution. Wisdom is knowing the balance," I said.

We entered the inn and spoke to the owner about our room and a meal. He spoke very softly to Me, saying, "If You are staying here tonight, take care, My friend, there are some dangerous people here." He looked from side to side and continued, "If I were You, I would stay in My room, and not come out until morning."

"Thank you for your advice, but we are hungry and need to eat," I replied.

"Well, be very careful what You say and do when You go to eat. There are some guests here tonight that I wish were elsewhere," he advised.

"Thank you for your concern, my friend. We will be careful."

We were then shown to the two rooms we had to share. We all gathered in one room where I said to My followers, "Whatever happens tonight, do not get angry, stay calm, and trust in Me."

I led My followers into the large room where the meal was to be served. Looking around I could see three or four groups of men huddled together in quiet discussions. Some of them looked up as we entered the room. I nodded polite "Hello's," and smiled at those with raised heads. Some responded, while others looked at us suspiciously.

When we sat at our table, the owner came rushing in with a large bowl of broth, which he put in the center of the table. Steam was rising cloudlike from the dish. Some servants then brought bread for us to have with the broth, and the owner leaned across the table saying, very softly, "Remember, take care, these are dangerous times."

I smiled at him, saying, "Yes, thank you for your warnings." After he left the table, I said to My disciples, "Let us pray to God in thanks for what we receive with this meal."

Together we began to thank My Father, but I could see how nervous some of My disciples were, and how this nervousness was making it difficult for them to pray. "Forget all else and think of God when you pray. Let all distractions disappear. Think of God's love for you, and what God does in your life. Then pray from your hearts with this love you have for God," I said.

We continued to pray and all their fears seemed to fade as they thought of what I had said. We then began to eat our meal, which was very welcome after the day of prayer and no food. One of the other men in the room came to our table and stood at the end of it. With his hands on the table, he leaned forward and said, briskly, "Who are you lot? Where are you from?"

Everyone at the table remained silent, and looked to Me.

"I am Jesus of Nazareth, and these are My friends," I said in reply.

"You are Jesus the Prophet? I don't believe it, You look so scruffy," he laughed.

"If You are a prophet, tell me what is my future," he said, as he banged his fist on the table.

"My friend," I said, "there is no need for anger, we are all sons of Yahweh."

"I am not Your friend, and I asked You a question. Are You a prophet or not?"

Peter made to stand up, but I looked at him and he stayed sitting. Another man came over and said to his companion at our table, "Leave them alone, they are harmless. We have more important things to do than this."

He placed his hand on his friend's arm, who shook himself free and bellowed, "I want an answer from this so called prophet, and I want it now!"

"My friend," I said.

"I am not Your friend!" he shouted back.

"You have been so frustrated, so angry with the occupation of our land by the Romans, you forget who your people are," I said. He stared at Me as if he could kill Me. I continued, "We are all Jews. We are all brothers. We all should be living the commandments Yahweh gave to Moses, for Israel was chosen to follow God's commandments, and to be an example of God's love in the world."

"The commandments! That's a good one," he said out loud. "Is it meant that only we follow them, but everyone else can do as they wish? Look what that has cost us—our land."

"God gave you this land, and only God can take it away. If you trust in God, you will find His will be done," I answered.

"I trust in my sword and my arm. When my land is free, then I will trust in God," he said, raising his right arm to show his bulging muscles.

"One day you will grow old. What then?" I asked. He just looked at Me. "One day in the future, you will be awaiting your death. Then to your surprise, your executioners will give the people a choice between you, and an innocent man, a choice to live or die. The people will choose you, and the lamb will be taken to the slaughter. At first you will be happy to live, but then, for the rest of your life, you will be full of guilt for the man of innocence killed instead of you," I said.

"There are no innocent men," he said, staring at Me with confusion in his eyes, "and I will take whatever I deserve," he said, bravely.

"You will wish you could have," I said. Again he looked at Me, as I said, "Tonight you have death on your heart...death and revenge. Remember the commandments Moses brought from the mountain. They are for you and for everyone. Thou shalt not kill is a commandment from God, and to break it is to condemn yourself to hell. God is watching you, and for every sin you commit, one day you will have to answer before God. Live the commandments, My friend, and live as God wants you to," I said, as I reached out and touched his hand.

He was still looking at me when one of his companions called out, "Barrabas, we must go. We have much to do tonight."

For a moment he wanted to stay with Me, but then he turned and said to his friends, "Another time we will do this work, but not tonight. Let us leave this place." There was confusion among the men he was with, so he shouted, "Come on, we are going!"

Within a few minutes they had left and the room was almost silent, until Judas spoke up, "That was Barrabas. He is a brave man."

"No Judas, he is a confused man." I said, "And a man who will carry much on his heart in times to come."

We finished our meal, when the owner came over again. "I am glad they have gone. They were trouble," he said.

"They were no trouble, only confused; but tonight at least, they will not bring harm to others," I said, standing up, as I started to walk towards the room to sleep. "If only they, and many others, would try to live My Father's commandments, life would not be so hard," I said, thinking how easily many closed their hearts to God's will in their lives.

J
E
J E S U S
U
S

Jesus ††† 7-6-96

I slept a restless sleep with thoughts of what lay ahead, and how Barrabas and I would be linked in the future. Barrabas, a man I felt sorry for, sorry that he had let anger, hate, revenge, and violence cloud his soul.

The next morning we rose and went to the synagogue to pray. The synagogue itself was very large and it was well attended, for when we entered it was difficult to find a place to pray, as most places were taken by others. A scribe was writing at the side as an important looking man was speaking, addressing those in the synagogue.

"When Moses brought the people of Israel out of captivity in Egypt, he brought them to a new life, a life that was to be God's. How many today live their life for God, and give their life to God? Not many, not many at all. How can we as Jews profess to be children of God, if we do not follow the commandments given to us by Moses? How can we claim to be the chosen people, if we choose to ignore God? How can many of us come to the synagogue to pray and be holy, then outside, live lives ignoring God's wishes?

"Today Israel is a lost nation...lost by its own will, lost by turning its back on God, lost in itself. What a shame is this nation before God.

"Now we must change. We must start to live as our father Abraham would expect us to; live as

Moses asked us to, and live as God wants us to live...as God's children, and show the world how God's love strengthens us, fills us, and guides us through life!"

He finished and sat down, the scribe stopped writing for a moment and there was complete silence as the speaker's words echoed in the people's hearts. One man stood up holding his gown on his chest with his hands. "You say these wonderful words, you say how many turn from God and live for themselves. Fine talk, but what about yourself? You wear good clothes, live in a big house, what about you?" he said, with venom in his eyes.

The speaker stood up, and said, "Yes, I have good clothes, a good house, and a good family. Yes, I am wealthy. These things my father left me, and I will leave my children, but they are no more than an inheritance I will pass on, as my father did. What is important is what you do with your wealth; how you share it with the less fortunate; how you give from your heart, and are .not afraid of losing what you have.

"If God has gifted you with wealth, you should remember it is from God's will, and use it to spread God's love. This is what wealth is for," the speaker replied.

"Ah, but you have so much of it, and even though you give much away, you will never be poor," said the other, loudly.

"I am always poor, poor in spirit because I can never please God enough, and poor in heart to see my brothers and sisters turn from God."

"Poor in spirit maybe, but your stomach is always full," jeered the other.

A voice spoke from the other side of the synagogue, "Nathaniel, you spoke well, my friend. Take little notice of those remarks from those who are jealous of you. Many of us know your good works. We know you help the poor, the sick, the needy, and that your house is always open to travelers. You give to the synagogue. You give of your money and your time. If only there were more like you," the man said smiling, then sat down.

Another voice spoke out loudly, "It is true. We all know Nathaniel is a good man. He always speaks the truth and from his heart. Let us reflect on what he has said for there is much in it."

For a long time there was silence until a young man stood up. "How can we bring Israel back to God then?" he asked.

Nathaniel stood, and replied, "By prayer and by living to God's will. Then you will turn the tide. It is when individuals change and return to God, that soon a nation changes."

I felt so happy hearing these words, and I saw in Nathaniel a true man of God.

"Jesus," said Peter, who was next to me, "will You say anything?"

"I do not need to. It has all been said," I replied.

Someone had heard Peter say My name, and a whisper went around the room, "It is Jesus. Jesus is here."

One of the elders rose, and said to Me, "Are You Jesus of Nazareth?"

"Yes," I replied.

"Would You speak to us?" he asked.

I stood up and read a Psalm out loud, a Psalm about David's trust in God. Then I sat down. There was silence, with all eyes on Me.

Then someone said, "Explain what You mean."

"When Nathaniel spoke, he said Israel needed to return to God's will, and live in God's love. This Psalm also says this, and it says to trust in God. Trust and have no fear for God is with us," I answered. Then I sat down and closed My eyes as others discussed between themselves the Psalm (Psalm 23, the good shepherd).

Nathaniel came to Me, and said, "Jesus, would You eat with me tonight?"

I opened My eyes and said, "Yes, it would be My pleasure. Do you have room for My disciples?" I asked.

"There is plenty of room. Bring them with You," he replied.

When evening came, we made our way to Nathaniel's home. Along the way we passed an inn full of drunken Roman soldiers who were making a lot of noise and singing at the tops of their voices.

As we came to Nathaniel's house, we saw it was very large, with big wooden gates in a large wall that surrounded it. The gates were wide open. Nathaniel, his wife, Rebecca, and his son, Judas were waiting by the gate to greet us.

"Welcome, Jesus, and welcome to Your friends. This is my family," said Nathaniel, as he introduced us to his wife and son. After the greetings, we entered the house where we were led into a large dining room. Two servant girls and a male servant were standing near the table, as Rebecca went forward to them, and placed her hand on one of their shoulders.

"This is part of our family as well," she said, as she showed genuine warmth to each of them.

We sat at the table. Then Nathaniel said, "Let us say a prayer in thanks for our food. Judas, will you start?" All three Judas' began, but then Judas Iscariot and Judas, My other follower, became silent, as they realized it was Nathaniel's son who had been asked.

"Lord, we thank you for the food you give to us in this meal. We thank you for another day of Your love, and we thank You for the love You have given us in our family," he said. Then together we praised God.

The servants brought the food to the table. Judas Iscariot looked disappointed for it was a plain meal, and he had expected much more from a wealthy man. When the servants had finished bringing the food, they, too, sat at the table to eat.

"Jesus," said Nathaniel, "I have heard so much about You. It is wonderful to meet You. We are truly honored."

"Yes," said Rebecca, "such wonderful stories. Is it true you fed thousands from a few loaves and some fish?"

"It is true," said James, proudly.

"Yes, my friends, it is true that God in His mercy fed those hungry souls," I said, thinking not only of those fed on that day, but of all those who would share in the food I would offer.

"God is so good," said Nathaniel, "how he looks after His children."

Judas, their son, spoke. "Jesus, I have heard of so many miracles that you do in God's name. How can others do this so as to glorify God?" he asked.

I saw in his heart the true desire to bring glory to God, and not himself. I saw a humble son, who, like his father, loved God and loved his fellowman.

"Judas," I said "if you trust in God completely and offer your life in prayer to God, then miracles will happen. It just takes faith. In faith all is possible. You have that faith. Believe in that and see wonders happen for God's glory."

He smiled, and said, "How did you know I doubted my faith?"

"I see how you doubt you have any faith, how you think your faith is not strong enough, how you want your faith to be stronger. I tell you this, if many had the faith in God as you do, evil would disappear from the world," I said.

"But at times I feel so weak, so useless. I want to do so much for God, but I never seem to be able to," he said, with a deep humility that came from his heart.

"You do more than you know. Your prayers for others help these people, even if you cannot see it. Sometimes you do see it though, do you not? Remember your friend, who only wanted to drink and womanize? How you prayed and prayed for him. Look at him now, he has changed. He goes to the synagogue, he has a wife and a daughter, he has become a good man, the man you knew he could be. That is a great miracle, and there is the strength and power of your prayers," I said to him.

"I didn't see that before. Thank You Lord. It makes my prayers mean more," he said, with a big grin on his face, as he saw how his prayers had helped his friends.

"Not all miracles are noticed," I said. "Sometimes it is only the spectacular, that people recognize. Often the important miracles of saving souls go unnoticed. So many people pray and think their prayers are not answered. If only they would believe, if only they would trust that God answers their prayers. Sometimes the prayers are answered in unexpected ways, or in ways that are so subtle. Unless you look you may not see God's hand at work, but at work it is. God answers the prayers of His children; it is just that the children often do not see it."

Nathaniel looked at Rebecca, then said to Me, "I have another son who died. He became a Zealot and he killed many men in his anger. He turned from his family saying we were too soft, that we should rise up with all of Israel against the Romans. When I spoke to him of peace, of forgiveness, he would not listen. He called me a foolish old man.

"Rebecca's heart was broken when he left us to fight against Rome. Then, only a few months later, we heard of his death during a skirmish with Roman soldiers. We never saw him again, and the last words he spoke to us were words of anger. How I wish it could have been different."

Nathaniel looked very sad, and Rebecca was crying. Judas, their son had his head down, but spoke, "I pray for his soul every day. I know God will look after him. He will, Jesus, won't he?"

"Prayers are listened to by God and God's forgiveness is limitless. Sometimes young men are deceived into believing evil is good, that killing is acceptable. In the fervor of youth it can be so exciting to sin, especially if you have been taught that you kill for God or your country. Many good people have been misled in this way, but God's forgiveness is for them also.

"Your brother, at his death, cried out for God's forgiveness for the pain he brought you, and for the wrongs he had done. He saw in those moments how he had hurt you, and how he had hurt God. Then from his heart, and in truth, he begged for forgiveness. The last words he spoke were his mother's, father's and brother's names. When forgiveness is asked for, it is granted. So you see, Judas, your prayers were not and are not in vain," I said, with tears rolling down My cheeks, as I saw their son's death, and as I saw Barrabas in the background, trying to help their son, but then run away.

"Thank you Jesus. Oh thank you!" said Rebecca, crying softly, but feeling peace within, knowing her son had been forgiven.

Over the meal, we discussed many things, and this family's love of God was so clear, even in the way they treated their servants, as if they were part of the family.

The evening grew late and as we made our farewells, Nathaniel said, "You are always welcome here Lord, and if ever You need anything, just ask." Then he placed a bag of coins in My hand saying, "To help Your work."

I saw he would be hurt if I refused, so I handed the bag to Judas Iscariot, and said, "Thank you for your generosity. It will be put to good use."

Rebecca kissed my cheek, saying, "Is it all right to call You Lord, for I feel inside I should?"

"Yes, I feel the same," said Nathaniel.

"And I," said their son, with the servants nodding in agreement.

"A heart full of God's love knows the truth," I said, "and the words come from your hearts." I went to the servants and said, "It is a wonderful family you belong to, a family of God."

They smiled back at Me, and the manservant said, "Every day is a joy here, and every day I will pray more for my family. Thank you for teaching us, Lord." The girls smiled shyly in agreement.

Then as we left I saw Judas Iscariot looking in the bag counting the coins. I thought, some people find it hard to change, and some people never learn.

J
E
J E S U S
U
S

Jesus ††† 7-7-96

Walking back to our inn, we prayed in thanks to the Father for the love in the hearts of Nathaniel and his family. Entering the inn, the owner greeted us and showed us to our rooms.

"Jesus," he said, in a quiet voice to Me as I was about to enter our room, "could I speak with you privately please?"

"Of course, My friend," I said softly. We went to another room where we could be alone.

"I don't know how to say this," he said.

"Truthfully," I replied.

"Jesus, when I was younger I killed a man and took his money. That is how I bought this inn. I didn't mean to kill him, I just thought to rob him but it did not happen that way. Now everyday I ask God for forgiveness. There is not a day goes by when I do not think of this man. I do not know what to do to make amends. I am frightened that if I say or do anything, I will be found out.

"Now I have a family, and it would break their hearts if they knew. Sometimes I want to leave and go to the desert to die so that I will not shame my wife and children. Sometimes I think I should kill myself in repayment of the life I took. Then maybe God will forgive me.

"Jesus, I just don't know what to do, life is a torment. It truly is. Everyday I see his face and I do not know how long I can carry on," he said, with a look of despair on his face.

"My friend, you are repenting every day. You see your wrongs, you ask for forgiveness, and ask from your heart. The sorrow you feel at your sins shows that you truly do want forgiveness. The guilt and shame you feel about your actions show you have recognized the evil you did, and now you reject it."

He interrupted, "Yes, but I still robbed and killed. How can God ever forgive me?"

"God's mercy is fathomless. God's mercy is offered to all who seek it. God's mercy is for everyone, regardless of what they have done, if they repent and do heartfelt penance," I said.

"What penance should I do, Jesus?" he asked.

"Do you know this man's family?" I asked him.

"Yes, I do," he replied, "but I avoid them, because I am so ashamed of myself."

"Make friends with them, and do all you can to help them," I said.

"They are poor now. Since he died their business has collapsed, and they live a poor life," he stated.

"Well, help them rebuild their lives," I said.

"But how, Jesus, without arousing suspicions?" he said, worriedly.

"Help them in any way you can. Do not worry about what others may think. Help them and love them as your own family," I advised him.

"I will, I will. You are right. It doesn't matter what others think or do, or if the truth is found out. God will know I am sorry, so whatever happens will be in His hand," he said, as he realized the truth.

"God knows already that you are sorry but now you must do your penance, a penance that will help those you hurt, and a penance that will help you. Penance does not mean to tear your clothes and cover yourself in ashes, walking around showing the world how you suffer. Penance is coming to understand what you need to do to overcome your weaknesses and fears that led you into sin. Penance is saying sorry to God from your heart. Penance is trying your hardest to make up for the wrongs you have done, and penance is accepting that you will make mistakes, and that the strength you need to overcome them is found in God," I explained to him.

"Thank You, Jesus. You are so wise. You have opened my eyes to what I should do. Now life will be a little easier," he said gratefully.

"Live your life for God from now on. Be a friend to all. Pray often, and offer each day in reparation for what you have done. Then accept God's mercy into your heart, and become a light burning in the dark," I said, as I reached forward and placed My hand on his shoulder. "When you do this, also learn to forgive yourself, or you may be trapped by sin again."

"What do You mean?" he asked.

"See how you thought to take your own life. Well, that would not have been any type of penance, for to kill is a sin. This is how evil works. Often it deceives people into believing that the repayment demanded of them is a repayment that is another sin. All this does is allow evil to grow.

"If you had taken this path, look also at the pain it would have caused your family and friends left behind. They would be suffering because of your sins. This is how evil works. Through what appears to be the solution to a problem, a solution that is no answer at all, it is only a millstone that hangs around those left behind, throughout their lives."

"You are right, You are right. It is so clear. Why didn't I see it before?" he almost shouted.

"Because in your guilt, you allowed evil to enter your mind and put thoughts there that seemed to be the only answer. Remember, God is the only answer, and God longs to forgive you. Once you accept God's forgiveness, let go of the guilt but remember the sin, so that you do not do the same again."

"Jesus, thank You. You have saved my life, my mind, my family, and my soul. I owe You so much. Whatever You ask is Yours," he said.

"All I ask, I have said. Do that and find peace, God's peace." Then I left to sleep. As I walked away I heard him sobbing and saying, "Thank You, Lord, thank You."

J
E
J E S U S
U
S

Jesus ††† 7-10-96

The next morning we returned to the synagogue to pray. We remained there all morning, leaving in the middle of the day to return to the inn. Along the way we passed two cripples, begging for alms. I turned to Judas and said, "Give them the money Nathaniel gave us."

"What, all of it?" Judas exclaimed.

"Yes, all of it. We do not need it," I replied.

"But Lord, we may need it later," Judas objected.

"What we need will be provided," I said, giving Judas a look that showed I meant what I said.

Reluctantly, Judas gave the money to the cripples, the older of whom said gratefully, "Thank You, master. Thank You, so much. We will share it with the other beggars who are in need. It is too much just for us two." I looked into his heart and knew he spoke the truth.

"Judas," I said, "you could learn from this man if only you could see the lesson." Judas remained quiet. I took the man's hand saying, "Your heart is full of love and compassion, love that comes from God."

He answered, "God, yes. I love Him so much, and I thank Him for my life, for even though I am a cripple and poor, God fills my heart with joy. I always feel so happy just to be alive."

"My friend, your love and your faith have healed you," I said. Then the man stood straight, threw away his stick, and walked normally. He began to dance and sing the praises of God.

"What about me?" said the other.

"My friend, do you think God would forget you?" I asked, as I put My hand upon his head and said, "Stand up and walk."

He struggled nervously to his feet, dropped his sticks and swayed back and forth till he took his first step. "Look, I'm walking, too," he shouted, and arm in arm both men danced in circles, praising God in song. My disciples watched in amazement as the two carried on dancing for some time. Finally they stopped and came to Me, kissing My hands.

"Thank You, Lord, thank You," they kept saying, over and over.

"Tell no one of this," I said, "and always remember how God in His mercy has healed you." They both promised, and then My disciples and I returned to the inn.

We ate a small meal which was filling and tasty. The owner offered us more but we declined. Judas looked very sad.

"Let us go for a walk," I said to Peter, and together we left. The other disciples remained behind to rest or to do as they wished. Walking with Peter brought me such joy, for his open heart absorbed what I explained to him like a sponge absorbs water. Sometimes, if Peter did not understand, he would ask directly and honestly for Me to explain something to him. Peter often reminded Me of a little child who, with wide eyes, wonders at what he is being taught.

Peter, a man who would be a strength for many in his example of obedience and humility. Peter, who through his human weaknesses, would show that even being so close to God, he still could make mistakes, even deny his God—then show how, in humble love, he accepted God's help in overcoming these weaknesses. Peter, what an example to mankind, and what a good friend of Mine.

"There He is," a voice cried. "He is the one who healed me!" All of a sudden there was a crowd gathering around us, so many cripples and beggars, the blind, the lame, the deaf, and the sick.

"Heal me. Touch me. Help me!" they called, reaching out with their hands.

"Peter," I said, "try to get them to sit down."

After some minutes, and with the help of the two cured cripples, Peter managed to get them to sit. Peter spoke out loud, "Try to be quiet. Listen to what Jesus says, and He will get to all of you." All of a sudden they were getting up and rushing forward shouting, "It is Jesus, it is the Prophet Jesus."

Hands were touching Me, and then a voice would cry, "I am healed!" And another, and another. Soon there were so many shouting for joy at their cures, they sounded like a choir praising God.

"Touch me, Jesus, touch me." It carried on until every one had managed to hold My hand or touch My clothes. Over one hundred were healed on that day, and then I was exhausted and said to Peter, "Let us leave now, I must rest."

Peter shouted at the top of his voice, "Jesus is tired now. Please make way so He can go to rest."

"Will He come back?" called someone.

Peter looked at Me, and I said, "Tomorrow."

Then I made to leave. Peter walked by My side keeping the people away, but they followed us to the inn. When we entered they sat outside on the ground waiting. The owner came to Me and said, "You had better leave and go somewhere quiet, or they will give You no peace. I have a house not far from here. If You leave by the back entrance no one will follow You."

"Thank you, My friend. That is a welcome offer," I replied.

"I will bring food to You later, so do not worry," he said, as he called a servant to show Peter and Myself the way. "What of them?" said Peter. "They must be hungry."

The owner looked at the crowd and said, "When you have gone, I will feed them, it is the least I can do." Peter looked puzzled, as he did not know of My talk with the owner.

"He is a good man," said Peter to Me. "Yes, he is, but he finds it hard to believe it himself," I replied.

When we arrived at the house, I went into one of the rooms to be alone with My Father. I started to thank Father for His mercy to Our children. I closed My eyes as I began to pray. When I opened them it was morning. I had fallen asleep, and My friend Peter had laid Me upon a bed and covered Me with a blanket. I lay there with My eyes open seeing My Father before Me.

"Jesus, My Son, after You have healed the people today, come into the countryside and be with Me to rest." Then Father showed Me a place at the bottom of a mountain with a small cave where I should rest. I closed my eyes and slept a little longer.

A knocking on the door woke Me. It was the servant of the innkeeper.

"The food is here and it is hot. You should eat now, as You did not eat last night," he said, kindly.

"Thank you, I will be there shortly," I replied.

"You probably do not know it, but there are hundreds of people waiting outside the inn for You. They have come from the surrounding villages as well as the town, and there are even Roman soldiers among them," he replied.

"I will eat a little, and then I will come to them. If you could, go and ask them to sit quietly, and say some prayers while they wait?" I asked.

"I will, but...uh, before I go I..." he said, slowly as he looked to the floor.

"Ask of Me what you will, and if it is in the Father's will, it will be granted," I said, as I smiled at him.

"Jesus, may I call You by Your name?" he questioned.

"Of course you can, for there is more in My name than you know," I said, as he looked at Me and smiled, uncertain of what I meant.

"Thank You, Jesus, but it is very personal. Can I close the door?" he said, as he started to close it.

"What is it, My friend?" I said.

"Well, I am a bit embarrassed to say this, but You being a man will understand, I am sure," he said, while I sat quietly, already knowing what he was about to ask.

"Jesus I can't stop wanting other women. I have a beautiful wife who also is a servant at the inn, and I love her so much, but when I see a pretty girl I want her. Do you know what I mean?" he asked, with a red face.

"Yes, I do," I replied.

"Well, I know You heal people, and I wondered if You could heal Me of this. I really do love My wife, but I can't seem to stop lying with other women. I don't want to lose my wife, but even though I have tried many times, I cannot seem to stop loving other women as well. If my wife finds out, it will hurt her deeply. Can You please help me?" he said, with a hopeful look on his face.

"My friend, it is within yourself to stop this. You only have really to want to," I said.

"But I do, Jesus. I do," he protested.

"Then every time you see a woman you admire, think of the pain it will cause your wife if you betray her. Then think of the punishment for the woman who commits adultery, how your fellow men would treat such a woman by stoning her.

"See also the commandments given by God to Moses, and see how you offend God by your actions. If you keep these in mind when you feel the desires for other women, then soon those feelings will disappear," I suggested to him.

"But it happens so quickly at times, the thoughts and feelings are there before I know it," he explained.

"Well, My friend, pray to God for the strength to overcome, and when God offers it to you, accept it," I said.

"Prayer, I haven't tried that. It might be worth a try," he said, rubbing his chin.

"Prayer is a powerful gift from God. If only you believe from your heart that what you ask of God in prayer will be answered it will be, if it is what is best for you. Prayer is often ignored but it is through prayer many graces and gifts are given. Prayer is a special time, for in prayer, if you open your heart truthfully, God answers. Pray and find your peace," I said, as I laid My hand upon his head.

"I will, I will!" he said, excitedly, "I am going to start right now." Then he began to recite a Psalm of God's love for mankind, (Psalm 41, Quemadmodum desiderat). I went to the other room to eat as the servant left by the main entrance, still reciting the Psalm and smiling.

Peter came in and said to Me, "He looks happy."

"Yes, he is, and today his prayers will be answered," I said.

We sat and ate in silence as I thought how evil could seduce such men, men who were good at heart, but were easily deceived into thinking that the flesh brought happiness, and forgetting about the true happiness that is to be found spiritually.

How clever is Satan that in the name of love, he can cause so many to slip into depravity, debauchery, and to treat their bodies as theirs to do with as they will, regardless of God's wishes. What a gift My Father gave when He created mankind! But, how easily Satan can destroy that gift through mankind's weaknesses. Sometimes the lonely of heart seek comfort in the arms of many lovers, but they never find it; they still remain lonely.

Many keep on the same path, and do not see there is no answer to their loneliness in what they do. The only answer to loneliness is to find true love, true love in God, which will bring comfort to the loneliest heart.

Sometimes in the search for excitement, respect, and stature, people take many so called lovers, and flaunt them to their friends, who then look upon them with admiration for the conquests they have made. The friends may then start to envy the one with many lovers, and begin to do the same. This is often how sin spreads, all in the name of love.

With true love one respects the body, and does not treat others as objects but for what they are, God's creation. With true love, excitement is found in each moment you spend with the one you love, together united in God's love. With true love, stature is not seen by who or what you have, but by what you share in love with others. True love, a gift from God...false love, a trap from Satan, a trap that many are caught by. So many weaknesses in mankind, but all can be overcome with true love.

J
e
J e s u s
u
s

Jesus ††† 7-12-96

After eating, we made for the inn. As we approached I could see My disciples encouraging the crowd to pray, but with little success.

"Where is Jesus?" the people shouted. "We want Jesus!" they cried. Someone saw Peter and Me walk towards the crowd. "Here He is," he called, and the crowd rushed towards Me.

Soon it was difficult to move with so many people around Me. Then I could feel someone pulling at My coat. I stopped and turned to see a young boy who was trying to get My attention. He had made his way through the crowd, and would not let go of Me.

"Peter," I said, "carry this boy." Peter picked the boy up and sat him on his shoulders. My disciples cleared a path for Me to walk through the crowd, and Peter followed with the boy. I went to the front of the inn, and gestured with My hands for them to sit and be quiet. It took some time but eventually all were sitting and there was silence.

I spoke loudly to them, "It is good to see you all here today, and soon I will pray with you and talk to you. I ask however, that you pray together for awhile, calling on the Father in Heaven to answer your prayers."

I turned and entered the inn with Peter and the boy, while outside Simon was leading the people in prayer and now they were following his words. I sat on a chair and called the boy to Me. He was only about six or seven with big wide eyes which looked at Me in awe. He came to me and I asked him, "What is it you want of Me?"

With the truth that children have, he said, "My mother is ill, and I cannot look after her. Mother sent me to You to ask for Your help. I know You will help because You are a good man. Will You help us?"

"My child, go home to your mother. She waits for you now, and she is healed," I said, smiling at his innocence.

"Thank You," he said, sharply. "I knew You would help."

"Son," said Peter, as he handed the boy some money, "here, take this coin with you. It may help."

"Thank you, too," said the child, as he took the coin and looked at Peter's face.

"You are a good man, also," he said, then left, as if what had happened was to be expected.

"Strange," said Peter, "he didn't ask any questions, he just accepted what You said."

"I wish all could trust in Me like that. He came with the belief I would help him. He looked for goodness, found it, and accepted it. The innocence of children, what a gift, a gift all have, but many lose."

I returned to the crowd who was waiting patiently. Then I began to speak, "I see today many different people joined together seeking God's healing and God's word. Here today are Jews, Samaritans, Romans, and Greeks.

"You sit here together in peace, together as brothers and sisters, together searching for the truth. This is how it should be at all times with all people, together in peace.

"Why is it that when you leave here today, some of you will return to your ways of hating others who are different from you, while now you can sit with each other side by side with no concern for race or position? It is because now you are opening your hearts to God, and asking for God's healing. And with your hearts open to God, there is no place for hate within.

"Can you not see this is what God asks of you...to love one another regardless of who or what you are, to love one another as part of the same family, the family of God? Love is the healing power of God, for God is love. If you can try to love one another, then you will find the world beginning to be healed by the power of God's love.

"Today if you are a Jew or a Roman or a Greek or Samaritan, throw away those names. Say, 'I am a child of God, and those around me are also children of God.' Then see you are one family, and treat each other as you would your brother or your sister. Love is a great gift from God, a gift that brings happiness and peace."

When I finished many were crying and embracing those around them. I walked among them and began to hold them, too. The love was so strong among these people now that I could feel their hearts glowing. This is the healing that all should seek, the true healing of the heart.

Just then a woman came towards Me with the boy, who had spoken to Peter and Me before. "I had to come and thank You, for I am healed, as You told my son I would be. Thank You, Jesus, thank You," she said, as she kissed My hand.

I looked at the boy, who stared up at Me, and said, "I knew You would, You are a good man." I reached down and stroked his hair saying, "Be good for your mother, and grow up to be a good man who loves God."

"I will be like You," he said, pointing at Me with one finger.

His mother said, as she wiped the hair from his face, "Lord, he is a good boy, and one day he will be a good man."

Then the crowd was around us laughing and crying, full of God's love. I started to touch the sick, and many were healed. As the day grew late, I made My way with Peter to the inn, and out the back way, to return to the house.

When we reached there, I said to Peter, "Tomorrow we leave, for I wish to spend some time with My Father."

"I will tell the others to be ready," Peter replied.

"Yes, but tell them we leave early," I said.

I sat alone for awhile, as Peter returned to the inn to arrange our departure. When he returned, he said with a smile, "The owner will take no payment. He says it is a gift, and the man who was here this morning said to tell You, 'Thank You.' He knows he is healed and all the desires are gone. Lord, You have done so much in this town. You have many friends here, even Romans."

"It is good so many have felt My Father's love. One day all will know the depth of God's love, but unlike these people today, not all will accept it."

Peter did not understand Me, so I said, "One day in love, God will offer His heart to mankind, but not all will accept it. Many will reject it, many will despise it, but in the end God's love will overcome, and many will be changed to be filled with God's forgiveness."

"Yes, Lord," said Peter unsure.

"One day, Peter, you will know what I mean," I said, as I closed My eyes and thought of the future.

J
e
J e s u s
u
s

Jesus ††† 7-13-96

The sun had just risen as My disciples arrived at the house. I was ready and waiting with Peter. We left the town as it was waking. People were preparing for the day, and there was the smell of food cooking in the air. We walked for some hours in silent prayer, each offering his heart to God in private, all except Judas Iscariot, who was thinking of the money we had been given over the past few days.

In the distance were the mountains. I said to My friends, "I will go into the mountains for three days. When we get closer, find a place where you can wait for Me."

Peter spoke, "Three days is a long time, Lord. Maybe one of us should go with You."

"My friends, I will be with My Father. I will not be alone, and three days will pass quickly," I replied. Peter looked at Me and said no more, for he knew I would not change My mind.

It was the middle of the day, and we had found an ideal place for My followers to wait. There was a small stream with fish in it, and on its banks plenty of trees for cover. It was an idyllic spot.

"I will be back in three days, do not worry about Me, and do not argue too much," I said, knowing there would be arguments, especially with Judas.

James came to me with a bag of food and some water. "Here Lord, You will need this while You are gone," he said, and he looked happy with My thanks.

I left My friends and began to walk towards the mountains. As I walked, I felt a chill in the air and I knew the evil one was near. I continued to walk and to pray to My Father until I came to the base of a mountain. There before Me was the cave My Father had shown Me. I entered and laid My belongings on the ground.

Outside it started to rain heavily, with a coldness in the air. I wrapped my blanket around Me to keep warm and continued to pray. Now and then lightning would flash in the sky lighting the cave, and I could see I was completely alone in this little haven in the mountain. The night grew darker and darker with the clouds covering the moon. Then before Me was My Father.

"Jesus, My Son," Father said, "rest here with Me." Then I could feel the warmth of His love and the cold seemed to disappear. I drifted in and out of sleep through the night. Then early in the morning, a man entered the cave and sat opposite Me. It was the evil one.

"Jesus, why do You live so? Why do You live in poverty and sleep in a cave when You could have so much more? It is not much fun being a king if You have nothing, is it?" he asked. I looked at him and saw the hate, the evil, and the wickedness hidden behind his kind looking face.

"My kingdom is one you can never overcome," I said.

"I will overcome, I will destroy You," he shrieked with venom. "You are a lamb. Well, I am a wolf and I will devour You," he said, threateningly.

"Begone, Satan," I commanded, and he was gone. How he feared the power of God!

I fell asleep for awhile, then woke to the sun shining into the cave. I went outside to a fresh warm day. The chill and the storm had gone with Satan.

I decided to climb a little way up the mountain. Then I sat and looked at the scenery. How beautiful is creation, a wonderful gift from My Father! While I sat there thinking of My Father, and how in creation He has given mankind all it needs to live, the Archangel Michael appeared before Me, kneeling facing the ground.

"Lord," he said, "I am at Your command."

"Michael, watch My friends while I am gone, for I know they will be attacked by evil," I commanded, with love. Then the Archangel was gone.

A little bird flew by Me, then back again. Then he settled on the ground before Me, singing. As he sang, another bird joined him, and then another. Soon there were lots of birds before Me, singing with such beautiful voices. This is the wonder of God's love in creation.

The sweet voices of love found in the birds' song filled Me with joy, but I also felt a little sad seeing how often mankind ignored the little miracles in creation before them every day. I reached out with My hand, and the first bird jumped onto it, and looked up at Me and chirped. Then all of his companions were either sitting on My shoulders, My head, or My hands. I sat there enjoying this moment of love.

Later when I returned to the cave, the birds followed Me and flew around outside singing such sweet songs to Me. I opened My bag of food and took out some bread, which I broke and threw on the ground for My little friends in reward for the joy they brought Me in their songs.

Evening came and I had lit a small fire in the cave, which I was sitting by as I prayed. I looked into the fire as I prayed and saw a beautiful dove rise from the flames. Then My Father was there and We united in love, the Trinity of Love.

My whole being resounded with the Father's love, the Spirit's love, and My love—one Love. When I was alone again it was morning and My friends, the birds, were singing an early morning song to Me.

Outside as I stood there, I saw the bird numbers had increased, and there were so many now the branches in a nearby tree sagged with their weight! The symphony of love they sang to Me, again filled Me with the joy of creation, and I smiled as I saw Father's love everywhere. I collected My belongings and said farewell to My friends of the air, who sang Me a good-bye song as I left to return to My disciples.

When I returned to the camp I could see they had been fighting. Judas had a bruised eye, Andrew a swollen lip, and Bartholomew a cut on his mouth.

"What happened?" I asked, but I already knew the answer.

Peter answered me, "Everything was fine until the morning after you left. Then everyone seemed to be arguing over the smallest things. Andrew, Bartholomew, and Judas came to blows. I thought they would kill one another. As I tried to stop them, I got very angry and started arguing as well, but then I felt differently...calm. As I felt this, everyone else quieted down and the arguments stopped. It was incredible, one minute so much hate. Then it was gone, replaced with a calmness, a peace. I don't understand it, but since then we are all friends again."

"Yes, Lord, we are," said James.

Then Matthew said, "It is unusual, Lord, to be so angry one minute, and so at peace the next. I was arguing with James about the size of a fish he caught, and I got so angry that I wanted to hit him. But now I am so sorry for that."

James cut in, "I was the same, Lord. I wanted to fight Matthew, yet he is my friend."

Judas spoke up, "I still feel a little angry. Look at my eye." How sad, I thought, that he still held on to some of his anger.

John asked, "What was the reason for it, Lord? Do you know?"

"My friends, evil attacked you and caused you to disagree, to want to hurt each other, and to have anger in your hearts."

Philip, who had returned while I was away, asked, "But why did it stop so suddenly? It was like the wind changed direction. One minute blowing evil, the next, love. I think I could feel the breeze."

"Satan was here, but My Father sent an angel to watch over and protect you," I said.

"Was his name Michael," asked Simon, "for I heard this name in the air?"

"Yes, My friend. It was Michael, a true Prince of Heaven."

Judas (not Iscariot) spoke, "I am glad he came. It was horrible here."

"There are many angels in Heaven. If you call on them to protect you and guard you, they will. Just ask them," I said.

"But no one calls on angels, nowadays," said Thomas, with doubt in his voice.

"That is so Thomas, but the angels are there waiting to help. You only have to ask. It is a shame so many people now forget the angels. Angels, who throughout time, have done so much for mankind... angels, who are the messengers of God, and angels, who are the guardians of mankind...rejected by many.

"But isn't this often the way with God's gifts, that they are rejected or ignored by mankind?

"When you pray, pray in love for your angel. Pray for his help, and pray for his protection in God's love," I said, thinking of the battle that had just been fought, and won, by Michael, a Prince of Heaven.

J
e
J e s u s
u
s

Jesus ††† 7-14-96

"Philip, tell us of your travels," I asked of Philip, who had been home to his family.

"There is not much to tell, Lord," he replied. "I visited my family and enjoyed seeing them again. It was good to be home, but I couldn't wait to be with You again, Lord!" he exclaimed.

"The love of a family is a wonderful gift from God. It should be treasured and enjoyed. Always remember, though, the love of God is first, for when you love God, then there is love throughout your life. All comes from God's love, so when you love God, you join in all love. This is how love grows and is spread," I said.

"Philip, there must be more," said Peter, anxious to hear what may have happened.

"There is, there is. The Lord's name is on people's tongues across the land. Everyone I met is talking of the miracles You perform, Lord. Many hope You will visit their towns or villages. Many wait for You to come," Philip said.

"If only all people would wait for Me to come, and then welcome Me when I do, evil would disappear," I said, with a sigh.

"Lord, we must be careful, for I have heard that many in the synagogues are jealous of You. Many wish You harm, and many wish You were not here," Philip said, with a warning tone in his voice.

"My friend, remember God is with us and nothing can stop us until My Father's will is done in our lives," I said, reassuringly.

"But Lord, You must take a little more care, or they will kill You," pleaded Philip, thinking I did not understand how grave the situation was.

"Life is from the Father and when it is taken, it is taken by the Father in His time. Life is only the beginning of an eternity of love, found through death. Death holds no fears, for it is the doorway to Heaven for those who believe in God," I said.

"Death is so misunderstood when it should be so clear. One day, however, I will clear the confusion for those who will listen, see, and believe. Then the truth of death will be known, and for believers it can become a joy, for disbelievers a sorrow. Death a gift to those who live a good life, and a sorrow for those who sin."

My disciples were quiet for a while, until Judas Iscariot spoke. "I am dying of hunger, let's eat."

Everyone burst into laughter and even I had to laugh at his comment. Judas didn't understand why we laughed, but he joined in, looking at us in a confused way. We then began to prepare a meal, and Judas gave a genuine smile now.

We finished our meal and prepared to leave when James came to Me and said, quietly, "Lord, Philip was worried about our journey to Jerusalem. He does not know if he will make it, as he has been unwell for some days. Did You see, he only ate a little, and yesterday I saw his stomach was swollen."

"James, do not be concerned about Philip anymore for his sickness has gone," I replied.

"Thank You, Lord," said James, with no doubt in his heart that what I said was true.

Later as we walked the road, Philip came to Me and said, "Lord, until You came today, I was feeling unwell, but as soon as I saw You, it was lifted from me. Yesterday I thought I would not be able to walk to Jerusalem with You, and that I may be a burden. Now I could walk to the ends of the earth."

"My friend. I am glad you are better, I would have missed you if you could not come with us," I said.

"Lord, I missed You when I was away. How my heart ached to be with You. At times I cried because I wanted to be near You," Philip said, shyly but truthfully.

"I am always with you, and I always will be. Take comfort in the times when you may feel alone, you may be threatened, you may be hurt, you may be in a place you do not want to be, or going to a place you do not want to go. Take comfort for I will be with you, and I will never desert you," I said, thinking of all those who would suffer for Me, even give their lives for Me.

"Lord, at times I could feel Your presence, but it was not the same as seeing You," Philip replied.

"Philip, you are blessed indeed, for you have seen Me. There will be many in the future who will not have seen Me, but will know Me; many who will give their all for Me, sometimes with only My presence to strengthen them. What rewards await them in Heaven, the rewards of being sacrifices for God; rewards you could never understand in this life," I said, seeing many being welcomed in Heaven by My Father, and being showered with Our love for eternity.

Philip asked, "Will there be many sacrifices, Lord?" I looked at him and saw his death, and the many others who would die for Me. "Enough, Philip, enough," I said, holding back the tears as I saw the love of all the martyrs, the love that brought light into the dark.

Peter joined us and said to Philip, as he put his arms around him, "I am glad you are back with us. I missed you, you know."

Philip smiled and said, "It is good to be back. I feel at home again." I looked at them and thought: two friends in life, and two martyrs united in death by My love. I began to cry out loud.

Both Peter and Philip looked at Me, and asked, "Are You all right? Can we help?"

"No, My friends, it is nothing. Do not worry. I am just thinking of how deep your love is," I replied as we walked on, with me crying and everyone else silent.

J
E
J E S U S
U
S

Jesus ††† 7-15-96

Within a short time we came to a village, which was draped in silence, with no one to be seen. There were no animals, no one, just an empty village.

"It is very scary here, Lord," said James, who had come over to Me, as we stood in the middle of the village.

"Are you frightened of the silence?" I asked.

"No, it is that no one is here," replied James.

"Do not be afraid. It is when you let fear take hold of you, that you allow evil to happen. Trust in God and be calm in that trust, for God will look after you," I said.

Just then we heard a scream a little distance away. "Come, let us see what is happening," I beckoned to My disciples.

As we headed in the direction of the scream, another scream was heard, then another, and another. As we came close, we could hear Roman voices laughing and shouting abuse. We entered a small valley where we could see the whole village assembled. Before them was a troop of Roman soldiers.

There were two crosses erected with young men on them, and a third man, who looked as if he had been beaten badly, was being placed on another cross. The crowd remained silent while the man screamed in agony, "For Israel."

As he said this, they drove a nail into his hand, and he writhed in agony.

"So much for this cursed land," laughed a soldier, as he stood over the cross on the ground, and spat into the young man's face. The cross was raised up and the centurion in charge of the soldiers stood in front of them, and barked, "This is what happens to criminals who oppose Rome. Remember this the next time you feel brave, and this," he said, pointing to the village animals which were tethered nearby, "is what happens to those who support them."

He signaled to his soldiers, and some of them began to slaughter the animals. The young man on the cross shouted through his pain, "They have done nothing, leave them alone."

The centurion looked up at him saying, "Willing to take all the punishment for your friends? How brave! Well take this."

The Roman took a spear from one of his soldiers, and with the blunt end, began to beat the man on the stomach.

"Stop it, stop it," cried an old woman, who ran forward. "Please don't hurt him any more."

The centurion turned and hit the woman in the face with the blunt end of the spear. As he did this, the man on the cross called out, "Mother!"

The woman lay semiconscious with blood running from her face. "This is the harlot who bore you," laughed the Roman, as he spat upon her.

The man on the cross cried out with a loud voice, "Oh God, protect my mother," and then took his last breath.

"God! There is no god but the god of the Roman sword," laughed the centurion, and his men began to laugh also. I walked forward. Then Peter grabbed my arm. "Lord, take care," he said.

"Peter, have no fear. Trust," I smiled at him, and Peter let go. I continued to the old woman and knelt beside her.

"What's this?" bellowed the Roman, as he looked at Me.

"Are you another son of hers? Are you a rebel, too?" he questioned, and raised the spear as if to hit Me.

I saw Peter running forward to help Me, before being hit by a Roman soldier, and falling unconscious on the ground.

As the spear came towards Me, I looked up at the centurion, into his heart. Then the spear stopped just before it touched Me. The centurion was as if frozen, when I said to him, "Would you like your mother to be treated like this? To beat an old woman is a sign of weakness not strength.

"Do you remember how your father beat your mother, night after night; how he laughed at her pain; how you wanted to kill him for hurting your mother so? Now you do the same. You imitate your father, whom you hated so much for what he did. Now you do as he did."

The centurion staggered back. "How did you know that?" he asked.

"I just know," I said, "like I know how you treat your wife. You follow in your father's footsteps. Yet as a child you swore you would never be like him, and now you are!"

"How-how-how do you know so much?" he said, nervously.

"I know about a young boy, who one night stood up for his mother, and was beaten almost to death by his father. A boy whose father locked him in a dark room for many days, with no food only water. A boy who said he would never be hurt again. A boy who, as soon as he was old enough, joined the legions of Rome and became a strong man. A boy who returned home full of hate and beat his father to death. A boy who has become a man full of hate and anger. A boy whose love has disappeared," I said, seeing his whole life before Me, a life now full of death and destruction, a life of anger.

He looked at Me so intensely. Two of his soldiers ran forward to beat Me, when he shouted, "No! Stop! Leave Him."

The woman was coming around now, as I looked up and said, "Remember your mother!" A tear formed in his eye. He wiped it away and said, "Gather your weapons men, we are going." He looked at Me, and said, "We will meet again."

Then he climbed on his horse and led his men from the village. I knew we would meet again, for in his hands, I saw the crown of thorns that he would place upon My head.

The villagers gathered around the crosses and lowered them, but it was too late. All three men had died. The old woman was crying over her son, as I walked to Peter, who was sitting on the ground with Andrew and John, caring for the wound on his forehead.

"Thank you, My friend, for wanting to protect Me." I said, as I reached down and touched his face.

"Lord," Peter said. "I will never desert you." I knew that he would, but I also knew he would become My rock.

I went to one of the elders of the village and asked, "Will you manage without your animals?"

"It will be hard, for there will be no milk for the young or no animals for our ploughs, but we will survive," he said.

"Judas," I called, "come here a moment."

Judas came to Me, and said, "Yes, Lord."

"These villagers need a little help in their time of trouble. Please give them some money." Judas looked at Me in despair, but did not argue.

"How much shall I give them?" he asked.

"Half of what we have," I said.

"What! That much!" shouted Judas, in surprise.

"Yes, Judas. They need help and we have it. There is no more to say."

"Yes, Lord," he said, as he reluctantly pulled a bag of money from his coat and started to count some coins.

The village elder spoke, "We cannot take so much. We can never repay You."

"There is no payment demanded," I said, as I turned to Judas, and said, "give them all that is in the bag. The other one under your gown is enough for us."

Judas couldn't believe it and almost cried, as he reluctantly gave the money to the elder.

"Stay with us tonight, Lord," said the old man.

"We have meat for tonight," he added sadly, as he looked at the dead animals. I saw in Judas' mind the thought he had: "At least we will eat well."

"No. My friend. We will leave you to bury your dead, and to grieve over your young men," I said.

Judas looked at Me in disbelief, as I said to him, "Tell the others to make ready. We must be on our way."

As we were leaving, we passed the old woman crying over her son, who lay in her arms. She looked up at Me and said, "He was a good boy."

I smiled softly at her and replied, "Yes, he had a good heart, and until the end he thought of you."

Then she said, "Did you hear his last words were to God?"

"Yes, and God listened and answered," I said.

She looked at Me and gave a weak smile, "He did, didn't He?"

The next minute she was shouting happily, "God heard my son, and answered him," to anyone who would listen. We left hearing her happy shouts.

How sad I felt within as we walked away. Sad that even after showing the centurion how he had followed a path of sin, it did not change him. Sad that so many would follow the examples of evil before them, even though in the beginning they would reject it. Sad that evil could draw so many into what they rejected, blinding them to what they had become.

I saw in the centurion so many who, abused in their childhood, would abuse others when they were older. How, instead of turning their backs on what had hurt them and embracing love, the love of God to help overcome their suffering within, many would put upon others the same pain, the same suffering they had been through.

Sin and evil passed from generation to generation. Sin and evil multiplying, growing, spreading through those who have suffered, and now are filled with anger, with hate. If only love was sought, evil would be stopped in its tracks, and the suffering would become the joy of love.

How blind is mankind to propagate what it knows is wrong, what it knows hurts, what it knows is evil, and what it knows should be rejected. It is a blindness of the heart, a coldness that turns hearts, created to be love, to hearts of stone...blinded to goodness, blinded to love, blinded to God.

There will come a day when the blindness will be lifted, and many will wonder how they accepted such sin, how they embraced evil, and how they hurt God.

J
e
J e s u s
u
s

Jesus ††† 7-18-96

Night was closing in as we settled under a large tree just away from the road. Judas Iscariot said out loud, "It would have been more comfortable at the village."

"Yes, it would have been, but they need time alone to come to terms with what happened today. Sometimes people need to share their pain among those who have suffered with them. Then together, with the help of God, overcome the pain within," I said, softly.

"But, Lord, surely with You there, it would have been easier for them," responded Judas, with a truthful wonder in his heart.

"I was there with them in their hour of need, and I helped when I was called upon. Now that these trials have finished and they have been helped through them, the villagers must find the strength within to overcome what lies ahead. It is in this way they can grow to become stronger in God's love, but they must want to and they must try to by their own efforts, and also by following God's helping hand," I explained.

"I do not understand, Lord. When did they call on You, and why can't You stay longer and help them?" asked Judas, still confused why we had left the village.

"Judas, the young man on the cross called for My help," I said.

"I did not hear him. He only asked for God's help to protect his mother," said Judas, perplexed.

"Yes, and I did," I said to him. "The villagers called from their hearts in their sorrow. I heard and answered them."

Judas was at a loss, so I said, "The reason we did not stay, was to let the people overcome their problems by their own means, and with the guiding hand of the Father. As they look to each other and within to lessen the pain and rebuild their lives, the villagers will grow closer together and will strengthen the bond of love between each other. As they look and see how God's hand is helping them in their lives, and how God helped them in their time of need, they will grow stronger in God's love.

"If we had stayed we may have been asked to stay longer and longer, with the villagers becoming dependent on us and not looking to what they have within, the gifts God has given them to overcome all difficulties."

"Yes, Lord," said Judas, in a bored tone. He had given up trying to understand. So many others, I thought, would be the same...others who would expect God to do everything for them, while they would expect to do nothing.

So many others who would say, "Why doesn't God do this, or stop that happening," instead of seeing that within them are the gifts God has given to overcome all difficulties. They only need to understand this and use these gifts, to find themselves growing in God and to be able to climb any hurdle that may be before them.

J
e
J e s u s
u
s

Jesus ††† 7-27-96

As I awoke, I looked around Me at My followers who were still sleeping. In their faces was the childlike peace many find in sleep. In sleep the mind does not block true feelings, and they are allowed to shine through. In sleep, often the dreams people have allow their true feelings, true desires, true self to appear.

The true feelings of love often surface as people dream of the good times they have had in life, the desires for love and happiness in the future, and the fears that it all may be taken away from them by their own weaknesses or by evil. Dreams are a reflection of life.

Lying there I began to pray, to pray for My Father's will to be done, to pray for the strength to do as My Father asks, and to pray for the strength My followers would need in the future. A little while later My friends began to waken, stretching and yawning.

Bartholomew spoke out, "What a glorious sleep that was. I had the most beautiful dream. I dreamt that I was in a temple, and all of you, my family, my friends, were there. Jesus was before us with His arms open wide, smiling at us. Then I could see His heart, and from within it came a warmth that touched everyone there.

"We were all filled with joy, and began to embrace each other. Then I saw each of you with your family and friends there. Then there were more and more people, who were the families and friends of them. It just kept increasing and increasing with each person being touched by Jesus' warmth from His heart.

"Eventually there were so many people millions upon millions all being filled with joy. All embracing each other. Then everyone knelt down before Jesus who now was surrounded by golden light. A loud voice was heard saying, 'Behold My Son.' I think it was God. Jesus' heart opened at the side, and out flew a beautiful white dove, which multiplied and was then hovering over each person.

"Jesus leaned forward and took the hand of His Mother who was in the crowd, and as she came forward, her clothes became golden with a crown appearing on her head. Mother Mary fell to her knees before Jesus and kissed His feet, and then she turned to us taking our hands bringing us to Jesus where each of us in turn kissed His feet.

"Then it ended, but the funny thing was, I didn't want it to end, I wanted it to go on forever."

"Was I there?" asked Judas.

"That was the other strange thing. You were the only one of us that was not," replied Bartholomew.

Matthew spoke, "Judas was probably collecting the money as the people came in."

Judas looked deeply hurt. "Matthew," I said, "it is not good to make comments that hurt others. Always speak with love and understanding, otherwise you may lead yourself away from the true path."

Matthew was facing the ground with embarrassment for what he had said. "I'm sorry, Judas. I didn't mean to offend you. Please forgive me," he said, truthfully seeing the wrong in his words.

Judas replied, "I am not only interested in money, you know. I love Jesus, too."

There was silence for a moment, then everyone began to prepare for the day ahead. I thought of Judas' words, knowing that he did love Me, but like so many others, the love of himself was stronger.

I felt sad for Judas seeing what lay before him, so I went to him and put My arms around him saying, "Judas, I know you love Me, and I love you dearly. Always remember I love you, and that I will forgive you any mistakes you make, if only you ask of Me."

"Yes, Lord," said Judas, who began to cry from his heart, but he did not know why. We embraced for some minutes, and then My followers came and put their arms around us, as Judas sobbed and sobbed.

"Lord," he spluttered, "I feel as if I have hurt You, betrayed You, turned my back on You. I don't know why I feel this way." Then he continued to cry. I waited for him to say, "Forgive me," but he did not. How sad!

Some time later, a meal was prepared and we all sat quietly eating it. My disciples were occasionally glancing at Judas, who now had stopped crying. I could see in their eyes the sorrow they felt for Judas, a sorrow of true love. Judas, who as usual was filling his mouth, looked around and said, "Stop looking at me. I only cried. It is nothing special. It won't happen again!" He could not see the love in his friends' hearts, he only saw condemnation. Judas so blind to love and in that blindness, only seeing evil.

J
e
J e s u s
u
s

153.

Jesus ††† 7-28-96

Walking along the road, we were singing Psalms and praying, praising My Father. When we finished, James was by Me saying, "Lord, as we walk in prayer, I can make each step I take part of the prayer. I time my steps with the words and in that way, even my walking becomes a prayer. It makes the walk easier, and not so tiring."

I looked at James feeling a joy within at the way in which he was growing in spiritual wisdom. "James, you learn how to make each action a prayer; what joy you bring Me in your love of God."

"Lord, as I pray I also see You in each word," he replied, honestly.

"When you pray, if you are open to the Word of God, this is what happens," I said, as I smiled back at Him.

"Lord, I feel so close to You with each prayer, and yet I want to be closer, so I try to pray harder but I never seem to get close enough," he said, a little confused.

"Do not give up. The more you pray, the closer you will get. Then one day you will find yourself united in eternal love with Me, and come to understand that it was your prayers that helped you get there," I explained.

"Lord, prayer is so wonderful. It fills me with joy. I feel so happy when I pray. It makes me wonder why so many people do not pray. Obviously they do not know what they are missing in prayer," he said.

"James, many people do not pray because they have been blinded by evil and so they see no value in prayer. Many people also try to pray, but because sometimes their prayers seem not to be answered, they give up and turn their backs on prayer. Others pray only as a duty, and put no love into what they say. Then their prayers are nothing but words. If all could pray as you do, in love, in trust, in faith, then they, too, would find the joy you do in prayer.

"Sometimes people are so busy with themselves, their lives, and their needs, that they find it hard to pray in love. This again is evil clouding their souls with self and closing their hearts to God. If only they would open their hearts and allow God's love to fill them, then many would come to understand the true value and joy of prayer, as you do. Prayer is a gift from God that can bring you all of God's gifts, if only you believe," I continued to explain to him.

"Lord, how can we get others to understand and to pray?" asked James.

"By praying for them, and by telling them of the joy you find in prayer," I replied.

"I will, Lord, I will," said James, as he began to pray earnestly for those in need.

How I wished all could be as open as James and see the true gift that is offered to them in prayer. Prayer, a grace from God, but seen as a burden by many.

J
E
J E S U S
U
S

(Note about the picture on the front cover of this book:)

In July of 1996, I was wondering what the Lord Jesus would want on the cover of *Through the Eyes of Jesus*. I was standing leaning on my desk when, from one of the shelved compartments, the picture you see on the front of the book fell before me. The Lord Jesus said, "This is the picture to use."

As I looked at the eyes of Jesus in the picture, I seemed to be drawn into them, and could feel the deep love of the Lord. This picture, however, is not how I see the Lord, even though it has some similarities, but I could feel His love from it. When the Lord appears to me, often I am overwhelmed by His love, His mercy, and His forgiveness. Sometimes I begin to cry as I feel the depth of His love for me and for all mankind.

I see the Lord with brown hair and beard, His complexion is slightly tanned, and He is tall. When I look at pictures of Jesus, none of them do Him justice, but all are similar as to how I see Him. The tenderness, love, and friendship I feel from Jesus is difficult to explain, as is a full description as to how He looks to me. I have not seen any picture that resembles Him completely, but as the Lord suggested this picture for the book, I know it is what He wants and for His reasons.